The lines on the palm reveal not only past and present, but also the future which lies in store for an individual.

This book is result of more than forty years experience of hand reading by Prof. Daya Nand Verma the founder of the Institute of Palmistry, New Delhi.

The subject has been explained with the help of hundreds illustrations so that you can learn to read the palm once you will go through this book.

Books of Institute of palmistry
By *Dayanand Verma* and *Nisha Ghai*

* Palmistry Ke AnuBhut Proyog
* Palmistry Ke Anubhut Prayog Part 1,2,3
* Palmistry Ke Vaigyanik aur Vavharik Sutra
* Palmitry Guide
* 50 Hand Print
* Shreemad Bhagwad Gita
* Bhraham Gyan Ka Yathatrth
* Dhyan Yog
* Mansik Samasyae Aur Ham
* Aane Wale Kal Ki Kahaniya
* Kalyugi Upnishad
* Nayi Soch Ki Kahaniya
* Zindabad Murdabad
* Garha Nakshatro Dwara Bhagya Nirman

Books In English

* Palmistry, How to MasterIt
* Fifty Hand Print
* A Handbook of Scientific & Practical Plamistry
* Palmistry Guide
* Stories of 2030
* How to Devlop the Right Attitude
* The Bahgwad Gita - Modern Interpertation
* Dhyan Yog
* How Stars Influence Our Destiny

All the
Secrets of Palmistry
for
Profession and Popularity
(Included Remedies to Remove Obstacles)

Prof. Dayanand Verma
Founder, Institute of Palmistry (Regd.), New Delhi

Nisha Ghai (Palmist)
Director, Institute of Palmistry (Regd.), New Delhi

DIAMOND BOOKS

www.diamondbook.in

© Nisha Ghai

First Published 1990
Third reprint 2003
Revised edition 2007
Reprint 2010
Reprint 2012
Reprint 2017
Reprint 2019

ISBN : 81-288-1617-9
Publisher   : **Diamond Pocket Books (P) Ltd.**
                X-30, Okhla Industrial Area, Phase-II
                New Delhi-110020
Phone   : 011- 40712200
E-mail   : sales@dpb.in
Website   : www.diamondbook.in
Edition   : 2019
Printed by   : Adarsh Printers, Delhi- 110032

ALL THE SECRETS OF PALMISTRY
By - *Prof. Dayanand Verma, Nisha Ghai*

Contents

Part IV : Important Guidelines in Practice of Palmistry

Part V : A New Concept
(A Clue to Physiologists to Study Human Nature through Palmistry)

Preface

I have been practising palm-reading for the past 30 years and have taught an innumerable number of students under the banner of the Institute of Palmistry.

My students belong to all sections of the society — they are industrialists, housewives, teachers and government officers — all very keen on learning and taking instructions from me. Some of the students are absolute strangers to palmistry, while others have studied books on the subject, but without imbibing the essentials of this science. All have gained from what I have been able to teach them.

The present work epitomises the essence of my study on the subject, my experience as a teacher as also my practice as a palmist. In addition, questions-answers have been provided which are commonly asked by my students. I am sure this book will benefit those who want to understand this science.

Whether you take up palmistry as a hobby or as a profession, all you need to do is to concentrate on the text and follow the directions given. Over time you would gain proficiency in the subject and be able to find answers to many questions troubling your mind on the significance of the lines and mounts on the palm.

As I say this, let me point out that there is seldom any science or body of knowledge in which man has been able to find answers to all his questions, because knowledge has no limit. Nor is there any limit to inquiries. The day we can find answers to all our questions may never dawn, because if it does, it would signify the death of science. Nobody would receive any Nobel Prize from that day onwards.

Difference Between General Knowledge and Science

The subject which you are about to study has not yet been

awarded the status of science. Some consider it as a subject of occult, while others dismiss it as hocus pocus. It is probably because of this that palmistry is not a subject of study in any of the Indian universities. But the present author and others before him have believed in the truth of this body of knowledge and discovered a scientific basis for its learning. Scientific formulae might not have been found, but there is clear evidence to show the impact of lines of the palm on one's life.

To cite an example, it has been known for thousands of years that wood floats on water whereas iron sinks in it. It is because of this phenomenon that boats were made of wood and anchors of iron. It was much later that science proved why wood floated on water and iron sank. However, today we all know why a heavy log of wood floats and the smallest piece of iron sinks.

How to Study the Book

This work should not be read like one continuous story, but one chapter at a time. After reading a chapter, repeat to yourself the salient points studied therein. On acquiring some knowledge about palmistry after reading three or four chapters, try to study the characteristics of your palm and jot down what it signifies, according to what information you imbibe, in a notebook. Read further and then compare the impressions of your palm with what is stated in the chapters you had read. After reading 10 chapters, study the palms of your family members and test your knowledge. But, do not read the palms of strangers till you have read the whole book, because, as the adage goes, a little learning is a dangerous thing. Predictions made on the basis of incomplete knowledge bring only a bad name to palmistry. If, in your eagerness to become a practicing palmist, you try to take short cuts, you shall never be able to understand this excellent science of palmistry.

—**Prof. Dayanand**

W-21, Greater Kailash-I
New Delhi-110048
Phone: 011-29242432

Part I

Scientific Aspects of Palmistry

I

Introduction and History

Palmistry has two divisions: (i) the shape of the hand; and (ii) lines on the palm.

The shape of the hand is an indication of the basic nature of the person concerned. Basic human instincts are: hunger, thirst, sex drive, anger, fear, etc. Instincts are basic to a man's nature and he is born with them. No process of learning is involved in them. *Chirognomy* is the name of the science which helps one to find the instincts of the owner of the hand.

The lines of the palm indicate the past, the present and the future of man. The science which deals with them is known as *chiromancy*.

The collective name for these two disciplines is *chirosophy*. It is also called *palmistry*.

We will first take up chirognomy and come to the lines of the palm later, because one must understand chirognomy before one can follow the significance of the lines of the hand.

The knowledge of palmistry was a well-developed science in ancient India. It was known as *Samudrika Shastra*. The practitioners of this science studied the shape of the various organs of the body and indicated the tendencies of that person besides forecasting his future.

A small part of Hindu palmistry in *Samudrika Shastra* was *Hasta Samudrika*.

Many of the treatises on *Samudrika Shastra* are now extant, but references to it are found in our scriptures which show how developed this science was in ancient India.

From India this knowledge was carried to China, Tibet, Rome, Greece, Egypt, Iran and other countries. The famous Greek philosopher, Aristotle was a learned scholar of both the branches of palmistry. Historians place his birth around 384 BC.

In modern times this science has developed extensively in Europe, the USA and other western countries.

It were the gypsies who spread this knowledge in ancient times. Gypsies are supposed to have travelled originally from India. Some western scholars took the gypsy lore of palmistry seriously and between the 15th and the 18th centuries many European palmists wrote a number of books on the subject.

Most of the scientific investigations on palmistry were done in the 19th and the 20th centuries. Some of those who are credited with taking the science to the drawing rooms of the aristocratic families are D'Arpentigny, a contemporary of Napoleon, St. Germain, Benham, Cheiro, etc.

The popularity of palmistry in Europe and the West in the 20th century brought the realisation to many scholars that it could not be dismissed as hocus pocus or black magic. They included Freud's rebel disciple, Carl Gustav Jung, who alongwith his own disciples considered it nearer to psychology than anything else.

Palmistry may have developed in India but most of the research on it has taken place in the West. That is why we will base our observations on palmistry as it is practised in the West. We would also refer to Hindu palmistry as discussed in *Samudrika Shastra* when and where the context demands. In the end, the conclusions would be based on our experience and study of the subject.

Let us now come to the shape of the hand and the lines on the palm and also how they came to be formed.

Palm Lines and the Mind

The palm is a mirror of our brain and mind. There are raised mounds of flesh on the palm which are known as 'mounts' in palmistry. They indicate the activity of the various centres of our brain.

The lines on the palm are the waves which indicate what goes on in our subconscious mind which has been compared to an iceberg. An iceberg, as you know, is 9/10 submerged in water and only the top 1/10 of it is visible.

The American palmist, Dr Eugene Scheimann has referred to many experiments of his times to say that the three main lines and the pattern on the skin of the palm are formed during the third and the fourth months of pregnancy (for three main lines, see Fig 1-A).

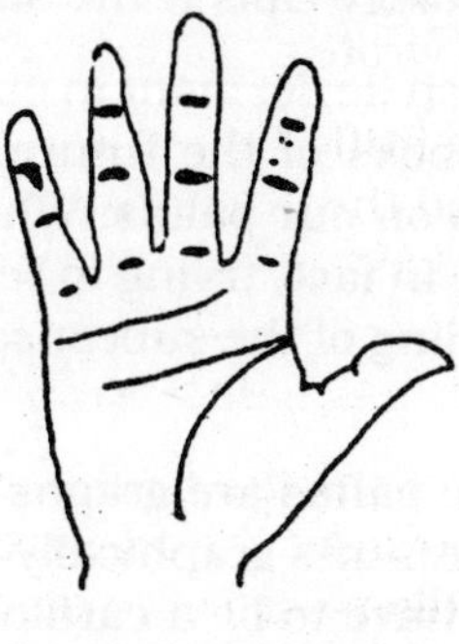

Fig. 1-A

You might ask: 'The mind starts functioning only when one is born. How do, then, these lines form at the time one is in his mother's womb?'

There are two answers to this question.

The Indian sages of your answer it to say that one takes birth according to his/her desires. When one's mind is free from desires of any kind, one attains moksha (or emancipation from the cycle of births and deaths).

From this one can infer that there is a time when the soul is in suspension, as it were. This is the period before man starts developing as a foetus in his mother's womb. It is the time when the bodyless soul is accompanied by the mind, and this is known, in common parlance, as pretavastha.

The second reply to the above question is provided by modern science. It does not believe in re-birth, but states that the genes of one's parents are responsible for his physical and mental makeup.

The qualities of one's forbears which lie dormant in the shape of genes are called *instincts* in psychology.

We may believe in the theory of transmigration of souls, or genes or subconsciousness, or not believe in any one of them. The fact remains that a child brings some qualities with him at birth. We have called the companion of the soul as the mind; psychology calls it the *subconscious*.

The desires which lie dormant in our subconscious mind are the building blocks of the future. These desires show themselves as lines on our palms. When we 'read' the lines of the palm, we are, in fact, trying to read the subconscious, because only a reading of the subconscious leads us to read the future.

The lines on the palms are graphs of the mind, just like the ECG which represents graphically the movements of the heart. Just as you have to be a cardiologist to interpret the wavy lines of the ECG, similarly you have to know the science of palmistry to interpret the significance of the lines on the hand.

When a person who is ignorant of the science of palmistry finds a palmist telling him about his past, his present and also his future, he may feel as though a miracle is unfolding before his eyes, but what the palmist is doing in fact is merely reading the subconscious mind of his client.

Palmistry is a science. Just as new experiments are being conducted every day in various sciences, old laws are being discarded as new ones are discovered, palmistry is also undergoing the same process.

Modern palmistry interprets the lines in a totally new manner; the old interpretations have been discarded. We shall give the old as well as the new interpretations of the lines on the hand in this work. And then we will come to what we have learned from our experience and study of the subject.

All the Secrets of Palmistry

Nature of Palmistry as a Science

We have just now called palmistry a science. But it is not a definitive science like chemistry, because it concerns the human mind.

Man is not only a body of bones and muscles; he also has a soul and a mind which are highly developed when compared to other living beings, like animals, who too inhabit the earth.

A cat will turn to a saucer full of milk, a dog would rush towards a bone and an ant towards a grain of sugar. They will not bother about a TV set, furniture or expensive jewellery because these things do not attract them. But, in so far as man is concerned, he can never be sure as to what he would rush towards and what he would ignore with disdain.

Palmistry is a science which concerns such a complex being as man. It is nearer to psychology than the experimental sciences are.

Unfortunately, palmistry has not got the recognition which psychology has. There is no university which teaches palmistry. The result is that people try to read the future of others without a regular course of study; sometimes, they say things which are so frightening that the listener tends to consider himself dead before he actually is.

A Palmist with a Sense of Responsibility

A Palmist is like a psychiatrist, but his responsibility towards his clients is more than that of a physician towards his patient. If a physician administers a wrong medicine, he may harm the physical body of the patient. But the harm to a man suffers when he hears that something inauspicious is likely to happen, is much greater, because the effect of a forecast of some impending disaster travels from the mind to the body of the listener. That is why we must delve deep into the profession of forecasting only after we have thoroughly studied the chapters in this book. There are no shortcuts and neither should you look for any.

Look at your hand as you study the text. After you have

finished reading the book and have imbibed its lessons, begin by studying the hands of the members of your family. That will help you gain better knowledge of palmistry.

The next step would be to begin palm reading of strangers. If you feel that something good is in store for them, do tell them. But if any evil is expected to happen after reading the person's hand, then first tell him how to ward it off. Without that, the science of palmistry is worthless.

We will come to the means to be adopted to ward off any impending evil in the further chapters.

Scope of Palmistry

We must discuss the scope of palmistry because it is to its study that we are devoting our time.

Just think, when does a man go to a palmist? Only when he does not know what course of action he should take. A client might want to know about the job he should take up or the course of study he should choose or the profession he should elect to follow. He is like a sick man who is unable to decide which physician he would consult.

A good palmist is dutybound to understand the problems of his client and advise him accordingly like a professional psychiatrist.

A bitter truth of life is that not everybody is fortunate enough to get everything that he or she desires.

If one's spouse is not to one's liking, or his employment is not to his liking, it may cause frustration to him. One's mental powers are used up in thinking about one's deprivations. If the unfortunate one were to consult a palmist, he might suggest something which might give a ray of hope to the sufferer.

The palmist must tell the cardinal truth to his clients that the lines of the palm go on changing. The speed with which they change is, however, so slow as to make the change unnoticeable. If the imprint of the hand taken a long time ago is compared with the one taken recently, you would notice the changes — some lines may have vanished 'and others

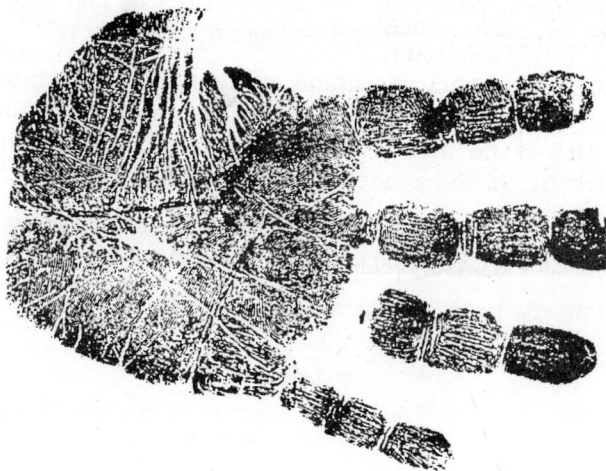

1-B

1-C

Handprints of the same individual

taken their place. *Figures 1-B and 1-C* are hand-prints of the same individual. The one at *1-B* is a decade old. The changes that have taken place in the palm can be seen in *1-C.*

Another cardinal fact which must not be lost sight of is that the fingerprints do not change throughout life.

The fact of unchangeability of the fingerprints indicates that to some extent we are slaves of our destiny, but the alteration of the lines of the palm is an indication of the fact that we are, to some extent, masters of our destiny.

The palmist should motivate his client to change his hand lines so that the inauspicious can be changed into auspicious.

How the lines can be changed would be revealed at its proper place in the book.

II

The Brain, the Mind, Environment and Lines

Quoting his masters, St. Germain says that all living beings are surrounded by a mysterious fluid which manifests itself in four types of forms: light, heat, electricity and magnetism.

According to Hindu scriptures, all things in the universe are made up of five *tattvas* (elements): *akash* (sky), *vayu* (air), *agni* (fire), *jala* (water) and *prithvi* (earth).

The mysterious fluid which St. Germain refers to is similar to *akash* in many respects, but his interpretation of it is entirely different from the one which the Indian scriptures speak of. The Hindus believe that it is a part of all living beings. It is the link between living beings and the stars and planets.

In addition to the versions given by St. Germain and Indian scriptures, I would also like to refer to William Benham who says that the current of life enters the human body through the first finger. It marks the heart line on the palm and then that of the head and finally the life line. The three lines are given in *Fig. 2-A*.

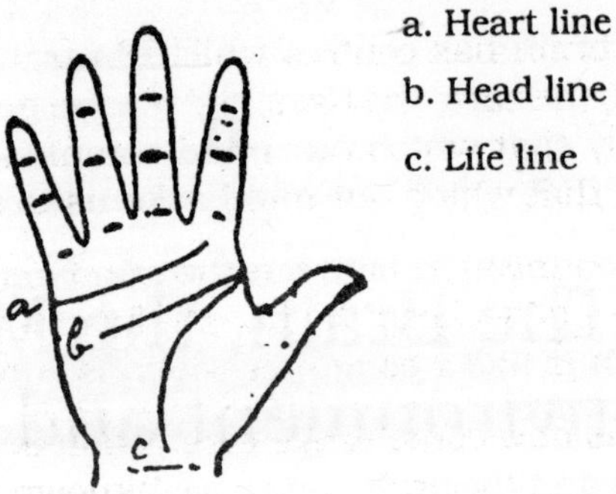

a. Heart line

b. Head line

c. Life line

Fig. 2-A

Benham says that the current of life reaches the wrist and then returns towards the fingers. In its return journey, as it were, it marks the Line of Saturn, the Line of Sun and the Line of Mercury. Then the current exits through the fingertips. We will go into the details later. The three lines are indicated in *Fig. 2-B.*

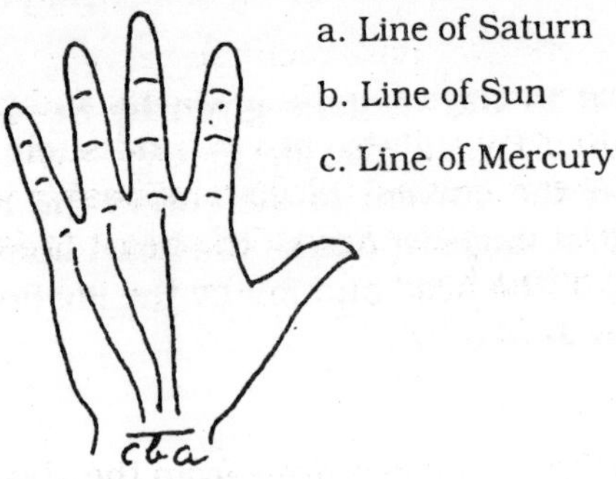

a. Line of Saturn

b. Line of Sun

c. Line of Mercury

Fig. 2-B

But the author has his own view about these things. And he has good reasons for his belief.

All the Secrets of Palmistry

In Chapter I, we said that the lines of the palm are like the waves of the mind.

The brain has centres which control the functioning of the eyes, the ears, the nose, the tongue and the skin, but we hear only that which our mind commands us to hear. We see only that which our mind asks us to see.

The connection between the mind and the brain is that which exists between the human fingers and the computer. The brain is like a computer which is run with the mind.

Let us now come to the connection between the fingers, the palm and the brain. It is a well-known fact that the brain contains many centres which control the functions of the various parts of the body. The vehicle through which this control is exercised is a system of nerves spread throughout the body.

The somatosensory area of the brain has centres which control the functioning of the various parts of the body. Large portion of this area controls the face, the palm and the fingers.

A lot has been written in the present century about the areas of the brain which control the hands. Palmistry has been expounding upon this connection for centuries, but the way in which palmists expressed their convictions was not scientific.

Faith-healers and holy men throughout the ages have touched ailing persons with their fingers and provided relief from their afflictions. The truth behind such cures is that the power of the mind has a close relationship with the brain and the fingers. Details of this relationship is given in the last chapter in this book.

Conclusion

The only conclusion we can draw from the above is that it is the fingers which connect the human body with the world outside. In other words, we can say that on the one hand, the various parts of the hand act as a magnet to trap the waves which emanate from the mind and the brain and on the other, they act as conductors for the waves from the world around us to reach the mind and the brain.

Let us recapitulate what Benham said: "The current of life enters the body through the index finger, reaching the wrist and on its return journey goes out through the fingers. This current is a constant phenomenon."

Through a process of study and cogitation the author has reached the conclusion that the index finger might be the conduit between its owner and the world outside, but it has no role to play in the formation of lines on the palm. These lines are a result of the waves which emanate from the subconscious which becomes active even in the womb and continues to be functional throughout life.

One cannot prove this fact in a test-tube as it were, but the formation of the lines on the palm proves that there is a link between the lines of the palm and the mind, the brain and the outside world.

By reading the lines of the palm we are reading the subconscious mind which, in turn, means trying to gauge the possibilities inherent in man. Reading the possibilities is akin to reading a man's destiny.

III

Examination of the Right or Left Hand?

A learner of palmistry is faced with the question as to which hand of the client should be studied before a prediction is made — the right or the left?

According to ancient treatise on Hindu palmistry, *Samudrika Shastra,* a woman's left hand and a man's right hand should be read for making predictions.

The author's view is that the left hand indicates the innate qualities of a man while the right reveal the changes brought about by the owner of the hand through his own actions. That is why both the hands must be studied, but more emphasis should be on the right hand (the active hand). This holds good in the case of women too.

An active hand is that with which a person writes; the other hand should be considered of minor importance.

There is no need to distinguish between men and women on this score. What the palmist should try to identify before he makes a reading is which of the hands his client uses to write with.

Most people work with their right hand and if the lines on the left palm are favourable and those on the right unsatisfactory, you can take it that your client has more inborn qualities but has destroyed his destiny with his own actions. If the lines on the left hand are infavourable and those on the right acceptable, it means that the person has improved his prospects in life because of his ability and talent.

To sum up, both the hands should be studied. Signs

which are similar on both hands can lead you to reach definite conclusions. But, where the signs are not similar, the deciding factor would be the signs on the main hand (the active hand).

Very rare are the cases where the signs on both the hands are similar. If you find such a person, you can be sure that there will not be many ups and downs in his life. If the signs are different, they signify many ups and downs in the life of such a person. Whether those changes are good or bad, you will learn on studying the book further and as you acquire practice in palm reading.

Part II

Chirognomy

IV

Map of the Hand: Terms Used

Every science has its own terminology or, to put it simply, it means the technical terms. Palmistry is no different: some technical terms would be used throughout this book and it is only proper for us to understand them before we go to the specifics of the subject.

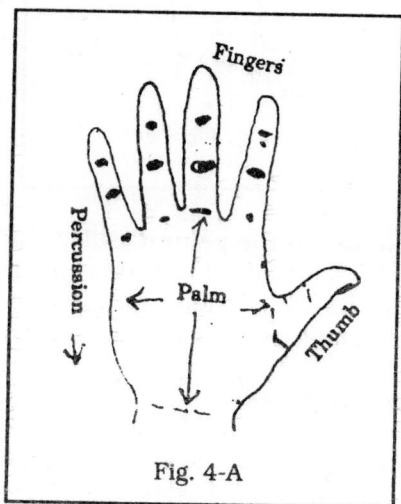

Fig. 4-A

Palmistry divides the hand into two parts *(see Fig. 4-A)*. The first part comprises the fingers and the thumb and the second, the palm.

The palm extends from the root or base of the fingers and the thumb to the forepart of the wrist. The part of the palm near the root of the little finger is called the *percussion* of the palm.

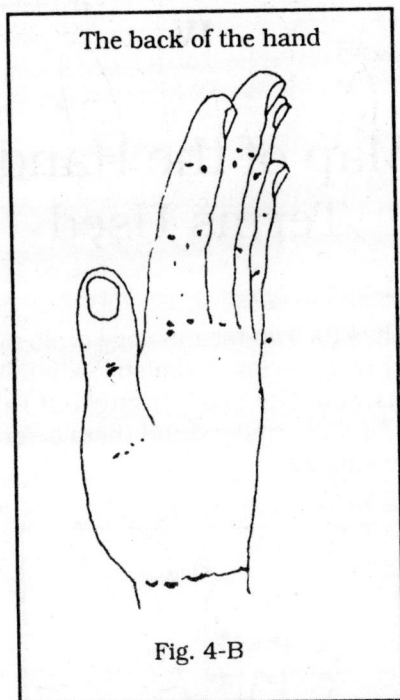

The back of the hand

Fig. 4-B

The side opposite to the palm is called the back of the hand (*see Fig. 4-B*). The nails at the end of the fingers are on the back of the hand. Modern palmistry gives equal importance to the nails as it does to the lines on the palm.

The Thumb and the Fingers

The *thumb* is the king of the palm. It acts in conjunction with the fingers because you cannot hold anything with the fingers alone. The finger next to the thumb is called the *first finger* or the *index finger* (*see Fig. 4-C*).

The finger next to the index finger is called the *second* or the *middle* finger, which is the longest among the fingers. And the one next to it is the *third* or the *ring* finger. The last finger is called the *fourth* or the *little* finger because of its size.

All the Secrets of Palmistry

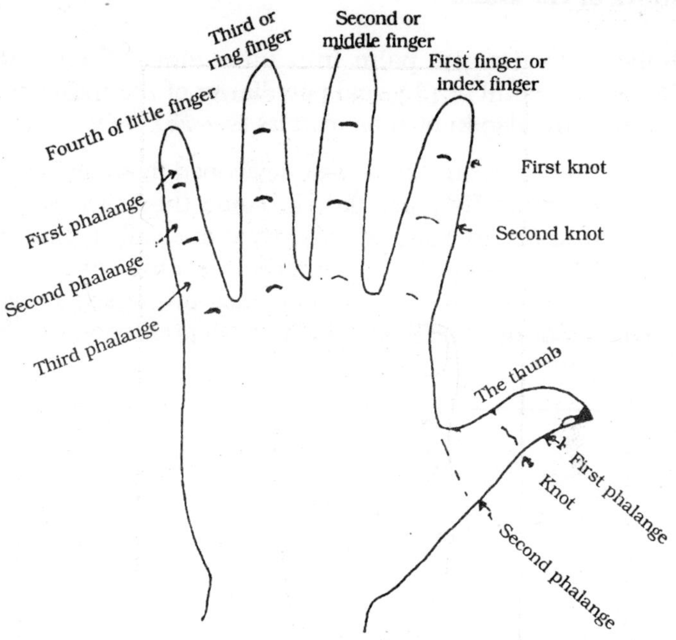

Fig. 4-C

Every finger has three parts or *phalanges*. The part which has the nails is called the first phalange, the middle one is the second and the one adjoining the palm is the third phalange.

The thumb has two phalanges — the first of them has the nails over it and the second one adjoins the palm.

Very few hands have phalanges of equal width. There are differences in the length and breadth of the phalanges. It is this difference which indicates the hidden feelings of the owner of the hand as also his disposition. But, we will come to this aspect when we discuss the fingers in detail.

Each finger has two knots — the first one is situated between the first and the second phalange and the second one is between the second and the third phalange. The thumb has two phalanges, with only one knot over it, when seen from the back side.

Mounts of the Hand

Palmistry divides the palm into nine zones. Each zone indicates a mental or physical peculiarity of the individual. The zones are also known as *mounts (see Fig. 4-D).*

The zones or mounts are well developed in some hands, though in others they are flat. In some they can be in a depressed state. In spite of this, they are called mounts. Those with prominent or protruding mounts are called developed mounts, while the flat ones are called under-developed mounts; the ones which are depressed are called deficit mounts.

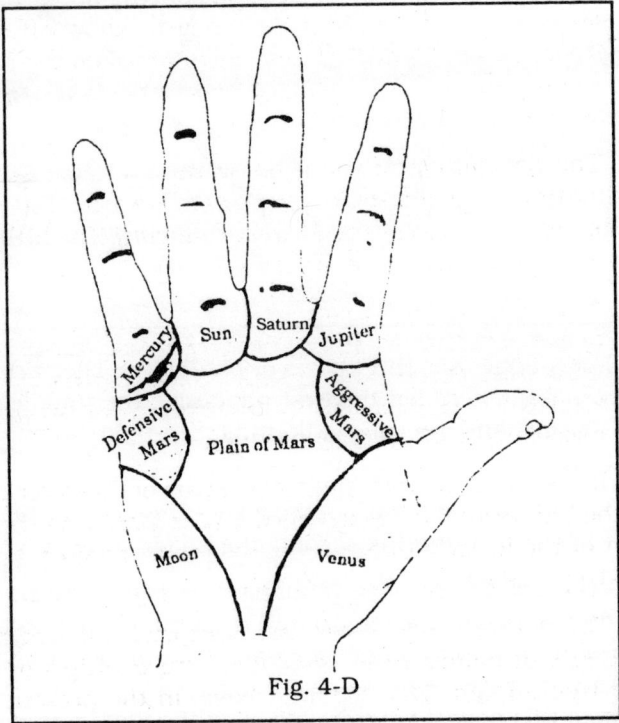

Fig. 4-D

The mounts have been named after the various planets. We will go into the details of these mounts at the appropriate place, but here we shall indicate their positions on the palm and some of their peculiarities to help you understand their role and also what comes in the following chapters.

The basal zone below the first or index finger indicates a person's desire for leadership, his ambition and his ego. It is called the *Mount of Jupiter*. The index finger at the base of which this mount is situated thus carries qualities of the planet Jupiter.

The zone at the base of the second or middle finger indicates whether a person is of sober temperament or not, whether he has the power of analysis and loves solitude or company. This mount has been named as the *Mount of Saturn*. The middle finger indicates the qualities of this planet.

The zone at the base of the third or ring finger indicates a person's zest for life, his tendency to show off and his desire for recognition. This mount is named as the *Mount of Apollo* or *Sun*. The ring finger has some of the qualities associated with this mount.

The basal zone of the little or the fourth finger is an indication of a person's pragmatic nature and quick-wittedness. It is called the *Mount of Mercury*. The little finger represents the quality of planet Mercury.

A small lower portion on the Mount of Mercury indicates the power of resistance of a person. The lower portion of the Mount of Jupiter indicates a person's courageous spirit and aggressive nature. In astrology, however, these two qualities are associated with the planet Mars.

In palmistry of the West, a small part of the lower portion of the Mount of Jupiter is called Lower Mars and the other part of the lower portion of the Mount of Mercury is called the Upper Mars.

The author's experience has been that it is difficult for students of palmistry to remember the qualities of Lower and Upper Mars. That is why I have, in the present work, made a distinction between the names of the two mounts. Patience is the defensive aspect of courage. That is why I have named the Upper Mars (a little below the Mount of Mercury) as *Defensive Mars*.

Bravery is also a form of aggression which manifests itself in the form of initiative a person shows in a battle. That is why we have named the Lower Mars, a little below the Mount of Jupiter, as *Aggressive Mars*.

This revised nomenclature would make it easy for the student to remember the difference between the two zones of Mars.

The zone under the Defensive Mars adjoining the percussion of the palm which extends to the wrist has been named as the *Mount of Luna* or the *Mount of Moon*. It is indicative of a person's power of imagination and a desire for change.

The zone under the Aggressive Mars, extending from the base of the thumb to the wrist, indicates the spirit of love, the vital force, sex and the degree of sympathy a person has. This is named as the *Mount of Venus*.

The zone lying amidst these mounts is generally depressed. It might be levelled in some palms to indicate the bodily strength of the person. It is known as the *Plain of Mars*.

More details would be given about the fingers and the mounts in the chapters that follow. The brief description given above is for the purpose of familiarising the reader with the names of the fingers and the mounts. The terms discussed here would be used with greater frequency in the following chapters.

V

Types and Characteristics of Hands

Palmists through the ages have categorised the hands according to their shapes and the placement of the fingers to indicate the basic tendencies of their owners.

The most widely accepted classification of the hands was done by the French palmist D'Arpentigny in the 19th century. It has been widely accepted by other palmists. His classification admits of seven types of hands.

Seven Types of Hands

First comes the *elementary hand (see Fig. 5-A)*. The palm of such a hand is small, thick and hard. The thumb is short. A person with such a hand is easily excitable, due to his brain being less developed than that of others. He is also subject to bouts of violence.

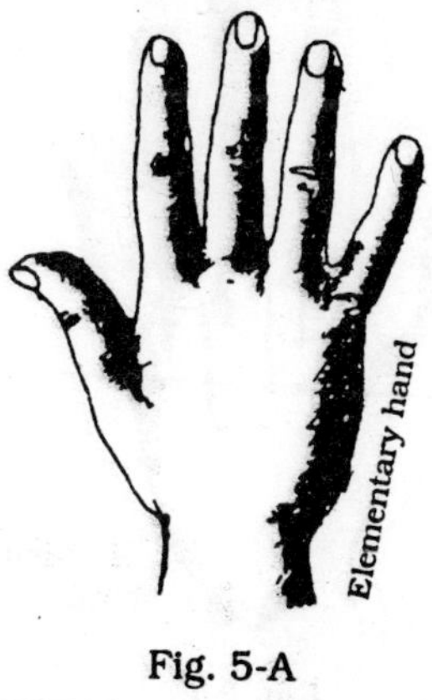

Fig. 5-A

The second type of hand is the *square hand (see Fig. 5-B)*. The palm of such a hand and the fingertips are square. People with a square hand are pragmatic by nature but show less of imagination. They are the ones who respect religion and law and order.

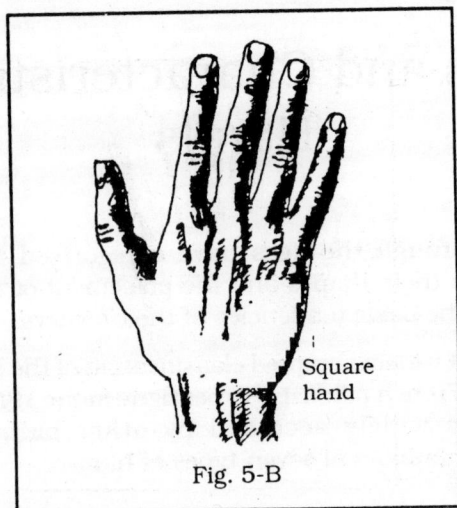

Square hand

Fig. 5-B

The third type of hand is the *spatulate hand (see Fig. 5-C)*. The fingertips of such a hand are spatula-shaped. People with such a hand have a zest for work, but possess less of stamina. They get excited easily and are generally unhappy and dissatisfied.

Spatulate hand

Fig. 5-C

The fourth type of hand is the *philosophic hand (see Fig. 5-D)*. The fingers of such a hand are generally long and the knots are prominent. Such persons are usually studious. Reasoning and analysis come easily to them, though work or action does not. They are thinkers and do not accept anything unless they have analysed it and found it to be right.

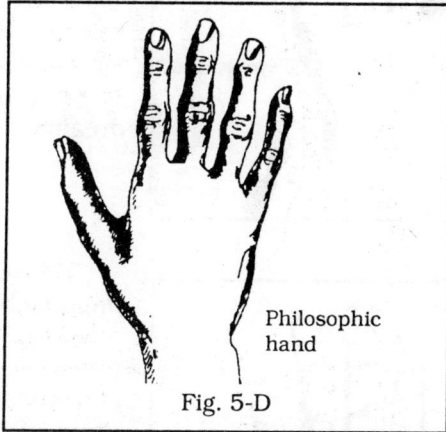

Philosophic hand

Fig. 5-D

The fifth type of hand is the *conical hand (see Fig. 5-E)*. The tips of the fingers of such a hand are rounded. Persons with such a hand use their hearts and not their heads. Extremes of emotion are a characteristic of such persons. They have an artistic bent of mind.

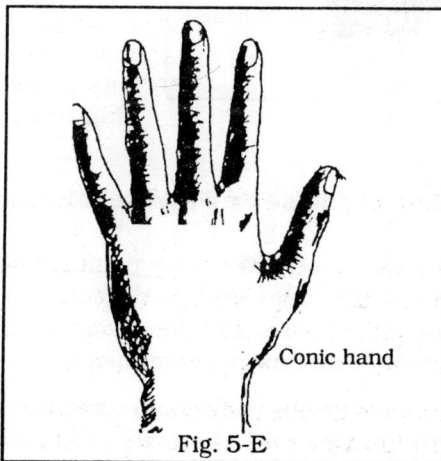

Conic hand

Fig. 5-E

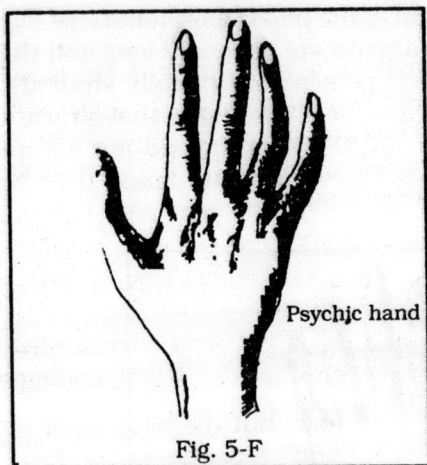

Psychic hand

Fig. 5-F

The sixth type of hand is the *psychic hand (see Fig. 5-F)*. The fingers are pointed and the knuckles somewhat invisible. Persons with such a hand do not work in an organised manner, their capacity for work being limited. They live in a world of dreams.

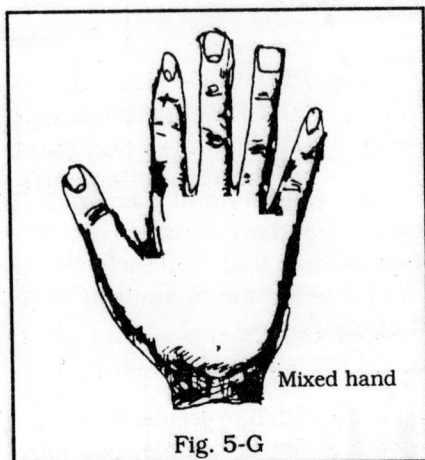

Mixed hand

Fig. 5-G

The seventh type of hand is the *mixed hand (see Fig. 5-G)*. This hand possesses the characteristics of all other types of hands; hence the nomenclature *Mixed Hand*. The fingers are not uniformly shaped; one may be conical and another square. Still another might be pointed. Such a person has versatility of character.

Categorisation of Hands by Western Palmists

W. Benham and the contemporary palmists do not place a hand in any exclusive category. On the contrary, they advise the budding palmists to study the special features of every hand about which we now propose to speak.

If the hand is flexible, the person concerned would show flexibility in his views and character. You can recognise a flexible hand by the fine pattern of capillaries on the palm which cannot be clearly seen without a magnifying glass. A person with a flexible hand has greater mental capacity than others. He is neither conservative not fixed in his views, but is always ready to accept new ideas.

Persons with a rough and hard hand are not generally prepared to accept new ideas. They do not make friends easily. The capillaries on such a hand are prominent and can be seen without a magnifying lens. Such a person is, generally, a good worker. His friendships and enmities are long-lasting.

If the skin of the palm is flexible, but the palm itself is firm, the hand is called a 'firm hand'. A person with a firm hand has both the power of thought as well as action. People with a firm hand think things out and take action to their logical conclusion.

If the skin of the palm is flexible and the flesh of the palm is not firm but soft like a sponge, the hand is described as a flabby hand. A person with a flabby hand is easygoing ease-loving. According to experience of the author Benham's categorisation is more accurate.

Thin and Heavy Hands

If the palm is thin and soft, the owner of such a hand loves money. It is not easy to read what goes on in his mind.

A person with a heavy and firm palm has greater capacity for work. If the skin over such a palm is flexible, you can assume that the person is adjustable. A person with a heavy but flabby palm is afraid of hard work. He is highly sensual and fond of eating, drinking and making merry. In short, he believes in enjoying life.

If the skin of a heavy palm is thick and rough, the man has no interest in art. And if the thumb of such a hand is short, the owner of the hand has no control over his mind or heart. He is given to violence. We will come to the peculiarities associated with a long and a short thumb when we come to the relevant chapter.

Broad and Long Palm

A person with a broad palm is more active, courageous and jealous. Such persons are quick to take a decision and proceed to implement it forthwith. If the skin of such a palm is flexible, the person has the power to think things out. On the other hand, if the skin is hard, the power of cogitation is limited but the capacity for action is enhanced.

Persons with long palms are thinkers who can analyse things and formulate plans. If the skin of a person with a long palm is hard, the level of his thoughts is low. Converse is the case when the skin of the palm is flexible.

A palm with much less width than its length is known as a narrow palm. Persons with narrow palms are deficient in courage, likely to remain unhappy and have less capacity to act as compared to others. Such persons are experts in formulating plans. Whether such plans would be good or bad can be found out by studying the other peculiarities of the hand, which we will discuss in the following chapters.

How to Categorise Palms as Long and Broad

One look by an experienced palmist is sufficient to categorise a palm as broad and long, but for the new initiates there are some guidelines which are given below.

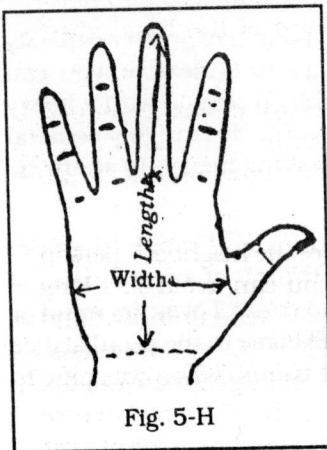

Fig. 5-H

The length of the hand is measured from the wrist (the line which separates the wrist from the hand) to the base of the middle finger. The width is measured from the line separating the thumb from the palm to the percussion (see Fig. 5-H).

The above information conveys the dimensions of the whole hand. In order to find the size of the palm, measure the distance between the base line of the middle finger and the first line of the wrist. This is the length of the palm and the width, as we have already stated, is the distance between the base line of the thumb and the percussion.

If we reduce the length of the palm by 20 per cent, we can obtain the width of a normal palm. In other words, if the palm is 12 cm long, its average width would be 9.60 cm. A palm broader than this would be a broad or wide palm and one less than this will be called a long palm.

How to Find the Average Length of the Hand

Now that we know how to find the width of the palm vis-à-vis the whole hand, let us find the length of the average hand in palmistry. It is tedious to measure the length and the width with a footrule; try to gauge the dimensions of the hands by looking at them. You can begin with persons you know.

David Brandon-Jones has laid down the following guidelines about the average length of the hands of males and females:

- The average length of the hand of a male who is 5 feet tall should be 18 centimetres.

- The average length of the hand of a female who is 5 feet tall should be 17 centimetres.

For every inch above this height, a quarter centimetre should be added to the average length of the hand given above.

If we follow this guideline, the length of the hand of a man six feet tall should be, on an average, 21 centimetres. The hand of a woman of the same height should be 20 centimetres by the same token.

It would be cumbersome to measure the height of a person to find out the length of his hand. You can avoid this long process by measuring the height of your acquaintances and also the length of their hands to get an idea of the proportions. After you have measured about a score of heights and lengths of different persons' hands, you would be able to visualise the build of every person and estimate accurately, or almost so, the length of each individual's hand. You would then know whether the length is normal, above normal or below.

How to Find the Disposition by Checking the Size of Hand

An average hand indicates the speed of work of a person and it would be average. Also average would be the standard of his work. If the hand is smaller than average, such a person is apt to view things superficially. He is not likely to go deep into the implications of what he does and will be in a hurry to complete it.

If the fingers of such a hand are short, the speed with which the man completes his work would increase but the thought that goes into its completion decreases. Long fingers with a short hand indicate that the person is more of a thinker than a man of action; the speed of work in his case is slow. We will go into the significance of the length of the fingers in the appropriate chapter.

Persons with large hands are apt to go into the details of everything and the speed with which they work is slow. But, if the fingers of a large hand are small, the speed of working increases; but if the fingers are long, the standard of functioning increases with a proportionate fall in the speed.

If a large hand is flabby, the person is easygoing to the point of indolence. If a large hand is firm, the person has a larger capacity for fine detailed work. People with very small hands are generally devoid of the power of thinking and those with very large hands have no capacity for work.

Colour of the Palm Indicates Disposition and Health

Those with a pink palm are jealous by nature, optimistic and sympathetic. Their hands are generally warm. This indicates warm-heartedness.

A whitish-looking palm indicates lack of warmth. Persons with such palms are cold, devoid of zeal and human sympathy. They are prone to be anaemic.

If the colour of the palm is deep red, its possessor is prone to be quick-tempered.

A yellow-coloured palm indicates proneness to diseases of the liver and he should consult his physician if the colour of the palm continues to be pale yellow.

Those with a tinge of purple in their palm may be prone to heart ailments.

All this refers to the colour of the palm. The colour of the back of the hand is darker than that of the palm.

Hair on the Back of the Hand

The back of a male hand is full of hair. If the hair are light black and are not thick, the man is likely to have an equable temper. If case of a thick growth of hair on the back of the hand, beware, because the man is likely to have a vile temper.

The back of a woman's hand is generally covered with a light fizz. If the back of her hand is full of thick growth of hair, she is likely to be like a man.

Advantages of Categorisation of Hands

If you do not get the opportunity to look closely at the hand of a person, but would like to find out about his disposition, keep the categories of hands in mind. By looking at a person's hand from far or by shaking hands with him, you can get an indication about his disposition. But, have patience! You must study the following chapters carefully before you begin to assume or predict anything.

VI

Fingers (A)

Long, Short and Normal Fingers

In the previous chapter we showed that short fingers are an indication of the dynamism of a person while long fingers are an index of his reasoning powers. But the question is: Which is a short finger and which is long ? This question cannot be answered till you know the average length of the fingers. Before we go into the various types of fingers, we will discuss the criterion on the basis of which we categorise a finger as long and another as short.

The average length of the fingers is decided in relation to the length of the palm. The point of reference is the middle finger with reference to which we can decide as to which finger is long and which is short.

We have already said that the length of the palm is measured by reference to the bracelet, the line which divides the palm from the wrist. The distance between the upper line of the bracelet and the base of the middle finger is the length of the palm. If you reduce this distance by 20 per cent, you can reach the length of the

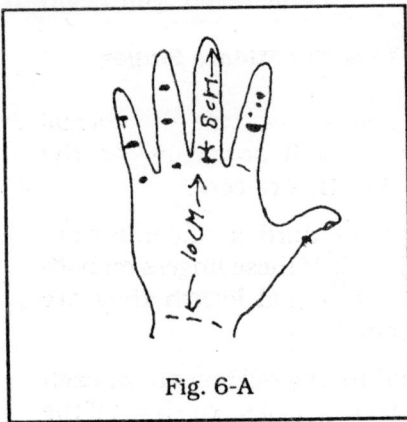

Fig. 6-A

middle finger. Using this criterion, if the length of the palm is 10 centimetres, the length of the middle finger would be 8 centimetres. This is the normal length of the middle finger (see Fig. 6-A). If the middle finger is longer than this, it would be called long for a palm of average length.

Persons with fingers shorter than normal have less of a capacity for thinking and reasoning. They are quick to decide and quick to implement their decisions. They do not go into the details, nor do they talk in detail. Those with longer than normal fingers go into the finer details of things and do everything with an eye on detail.

The reason why a man with short fingers decides fast is that he takes an overall view of things to arrive at a decision. They are the hasty ones. If the thumb of such a person or his palm is long, such haste is not harmful. But short fingers with a broad palm presage dangerous consequences of such haste.

Those with longer than normal fingers think for long before arriving at a decision. If the palm is broad in such cases, the speed of action is fast. But if the long fingers are accompanied by a long palm, the plans of such persons are likely to remain in cold storage for quite some time. If, in a business, persons with long and those with short fingers enter into a partnership, it is likely to be safe. If the long fingers are knotty, then the analytical powers of the person are enhanced.

Length of Other Fingers vis-à-vis the Middle Finger

We have learnt the rule by which we measure the normal length of the middle finger. We will now come to the measurement of the length of the other fingers.

The first or index finger and the third or ring finger are slightly shorter than the middle one. If these fingers on both sides of the middle finger are of equal length they are considered to be of normal length.

If the middle finger is equal to any of the two on each side of it, the middle finger would be considered short. If the ring finger is as long as the middle one, it would be considered to be long. If the middle finger is much longer than both the index and the ring finger, it would be considered longer than usual. The author has not come across a case where the middle finger was shorter than the two on both sides of it, but palmists are of the view that the possessor of such a middle finger is of mean nature.

Setting of Fingers on the Palm

We have talked of the mounts found at the base of the fingers — Mount of Jupiter on the base of the index finger, the Mount of Saturn on the base of the middle finger, the Mount of Sun at the base of the third finger and the Mount of Mercury on the base of the little finger.

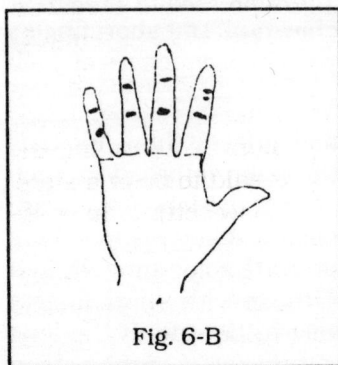

Fig. 6-B

If the bases of all the fingers are in a straight line, they are called to be in an even setting (see Fig. 6-B). Such a setting is rare. However. in such cases the person has immense self-confidence.

The second type of setting of the fingers is of an arch type. In this position, the bases of the second and the third finger are in a straight line and the first and last fingers are a little below but in a straight line. In an arch type of setting the special features of the Sun and Saturn are prominent while those of Jupiter and Mercury are subdued (see Fig. 6-C). The possessor of such a hand is a person with a balanced mind.

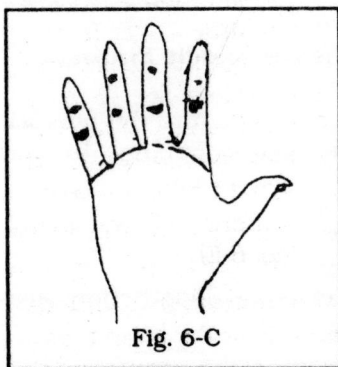

Fig. 6-C

If the base of a finger is higher than others or lower than others, the setting is called on odd setting.

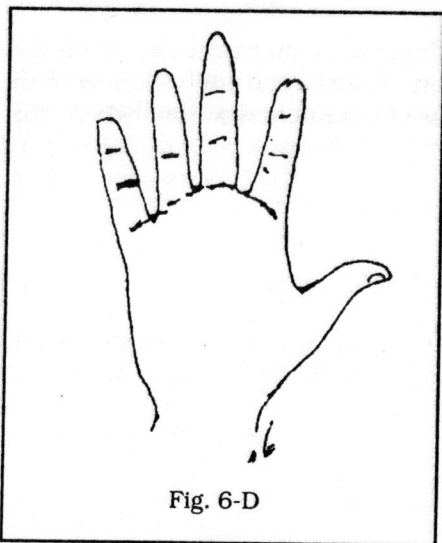

Fig. 6-D

In an odd setting, the finger with a higher base is called a finger with a high setting. The mount at the base of such a finger has a larger area and even if it is depressed, it is supposed to be developed. Normally, the middle finger is found to be in a high setting (see Fig. 6-D). If the Mount of Saturn in a hand is found to be depressed, it should be taken to be developed.

A finger which has a base lower than those of other fingers is said to be in a state of low setting. In such a condition the influence of the mount under that finger is reduced. The little finger is normally found in low setting. If the little finger is in a low setting, the Mount of Mercury has a smaller area and even if it is developed, it should be considered underdeveloped (see Fig. 6-E).

Fig. 6-E

We have broadly indicated the characteristics of various fingers and the significance of the mounts underneath them. We will go into further details in the next chapter.

Knots on Fingers

Each finger has two knots, while the thumb has only one (see Fig. 6-F). It is because of the knots that the fingers may be bent inwards.

Fig. 6-F

Knots are prominent in some fingers and not so in others. Those with prominent knots are known possess knotty fingers (see Fig. 6-G). Fingers without prominent knots are called soft fingers (see Fig. 6-H).

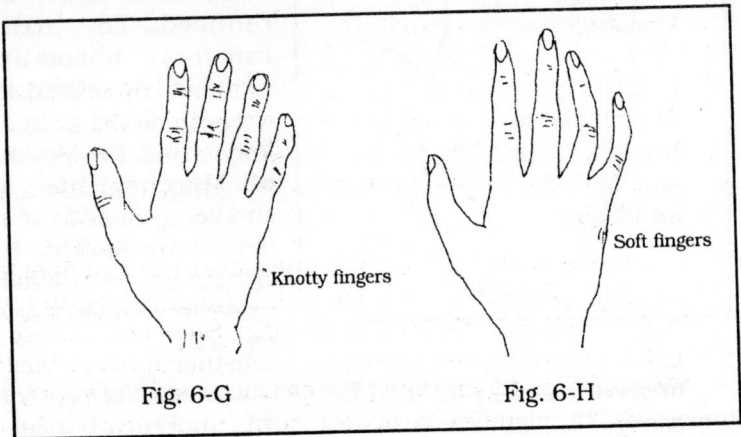

Fig. 6-G   Fig. 6-H

Knotty fingers indicate an attentive and observant person who is curious to know everything around him. Such a person has the capacity to think, analyse and argue things to their logical conclusion. But he is not fast to act.

Persons with soft fingers act under the influence of intution; they can be swayed by emotion. Such persons do not bother to think things out.

The knot between the first and the second phalange is called the first or *psychic knot*. If this is prominent, the person has a lot of mental energy. Such persons act intuitively and do not reason out their actions.

The knot between the second and the third phalange of a finger is called the second or the *practical knot*. A person with a prominent second knot is given to cognitive thinking. He delves deep into things and has an analytical bent of mind.

If the fingers are very soft, they look beautiful but a person with soft fingers is a dreamer who lives far from the real world.

The fingers — if they are too knotty — turn a person into a hard-hearted one. For the knot on the thumb, see the chapter on the thumb.

Phalanges of the Fingers

Each finger, as we have already stated, has three phalanges. The phalanges are not of uniform length or thickness. The first phalange indicates the emotional state of a person. If it is longer, the person is likely to be sentimental and a bit of an idealist.

The second phalange is the measure of the common sense a person possesses. If the second phalange is long and thick, it indicates that the person is tactful. Such persons are able to keep those around them happy, whether at home, business or service. Such persons are able to win condifence of friends easily.

The third phalange is an indication of the desire of the individual for physical happiness. If it is long and thick, the person is liable to be an easy and carefree person, given to the pleasures of life.

In the next chapter we shall go into the details of the characteristics of each finger. But at a glance you can easily see the type of fingers a person has and thus get an inkling of his nature.

VII

Fingers (B)

Detailed Description of Each finger

The Index Finger

The first or index finger represents the ego of a person and is an indication of his qualities of leadership *(see Fig. 7-A)*. A peculiarity of this finger is that it can be extended alone without the other fingers of the hand moving one bit.

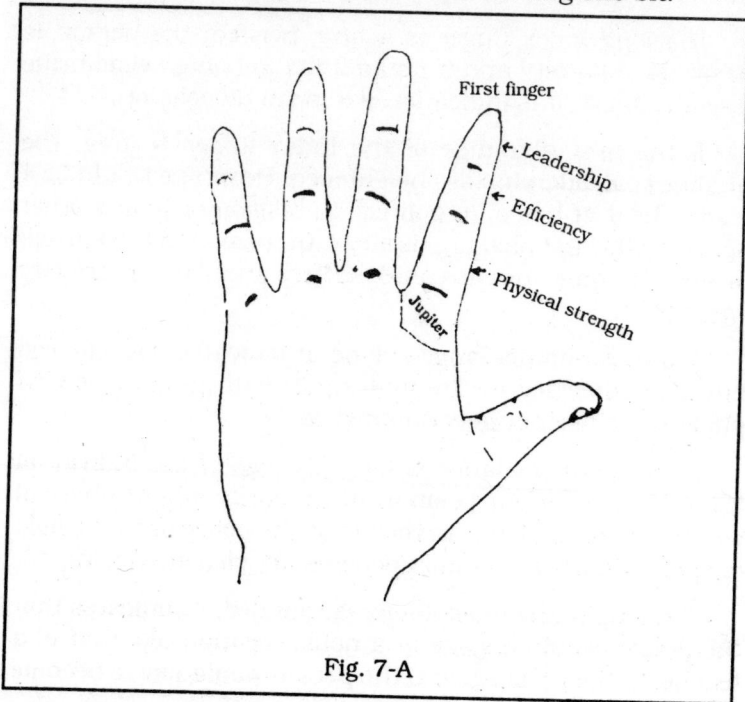

Fig. 7-A

At the base of the index finger is the Mount of Jupiter. It represents the characteristics of Jupiter. If it is a little shorter than the middle finger and almost equal in length to the third finger, it can be said to be of normal length. The normal length of the index finger means that its possessor expects respect from others.

If it is longer than normal, the person wants not only respect but also power and authority. Persons with such a finger know how to carry out their duties and to act responsibly.

If the index finger is shorter than normal, the person tends to shy away from responsibility. He is a follower rather than a leader and his life is without any ambition.

If the index finger is equal in length to the ring or third finger, it tends to bring fame and honour to the person. If it is longer than the ring finger, it tends to increase the desire in the person for complete domination over others. If it is shorter than the ring finger, the person suffers from an inferiority complex.

If a long index finger is a little twisted, the person is desirous of flattery and if, in addition to being twisted, the finger is short, it is indicative of a mean disposition.

If the first phalange of the index finger is long, the qualities of leadership are heightened. He or she would be a leader, be it at home, in politics, in religion or in any other sphere. If the first phalange is short, the person hides himself, is shy to come forward and suffers from an inferiority complex.

If the second phalange is long, it indicates not only ego but also efficiency in the individual. With a short second phalange, efficiency gets diminished.

If the third phalange is long, the ego of the individual leads him to seek a position of authority where physical strength is needed, e.g. in the army, the police or in the field of sports. In addition, such persons are pleasure loving.

If the tip of the index finger is rounded, it indicates that the person would engage in a noble vocation like that of a teacher. If the tip is square, the person would like to become a judge or a lawyer so that he can satisfy not only his ego, but also earn a considerable amount of money. Persons with spatulate-tipped index finger are talkative and love to boast.

Rare is a hand in which the tip of the index finger is pointed. In such cases, there is the desire to become a leader in the spiritual field.

If the setting of the index finger is even, its qualities are balanced. If the setting is low, it should be treated like a short index finger; if its high, it has the same qualities as a long one. We have already discussed the setting of the fingers in the previous chapter to which a student can refer while studying this book.

The Second or Middle Finger

This is called the *finger of balance*. On one side is the index finger which represents ego and on the other, the ring finger which denotes self-expression. Lying between them, the middle finger strikes a balance between ego and self-expression *(see Fig. 7-B)*. At the base of the middle finger lies the Mount of Saturn and it, therefore, represents all the qualities of Saturn.

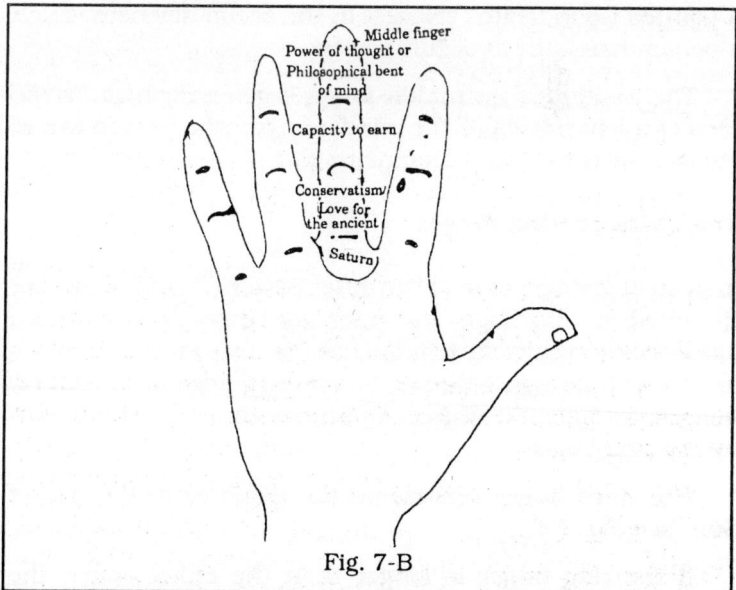

Fig. 7-B

A middle finger slightly larger than the index and ring fingers is considered to be normal. Persons with a normally long middle finger are intelligent, sober and steady. If it is longer than normal, the person does not want to mix with people and runs away from social contact. He loves solitude.

A person with a middle finger shorter than normal does not have sobriety; flippancy is his hallmark. It also indicates miserliness. A twisted middle finger is short, it indicates bad luck.

If the first phalange of the middle finger is long the person has the tendency to become philosophical: if short, it indicates lack in power of thought.

If the second phalange is long, the person thinks of making money. He might be interested in dealing in antiques. Desire for money is a predominant feature of such a finger.

If the third phalange is long, the person believes in conventions and loves to abide by old ideas and traditions.

If the tip of the middle finger is square, the person has a considerable understanding of law. A rounded tip indicates interest in mathematics, finance and trade. A person with a spatula-tipped middle finger is devoid of seriousness, sobriety. A pointed tip indicates interest in the occult sciences. Such a person has faith in occult powers.

The position of the middle finger is generally high. In the case of a low setting of the middle finger, the person would remain depressed and disappointed.

The Third or Ring Finger

Instead of giving a clue to the inner powers of an individual, the third or ring finger indicates his response to external influences and capacity to influence the environment in which he lives. A person's desire to impress others, to exhibit himself, for fame, the degree of enthusiasm — all are indicated by the ring finger.

The third finger represents the qualities of the planet Sun *(see Fig. 7-C)*.

If the ring finger is longer than the index finger, the

All the Secrets of Palmistry

amount of self-confidence in a person increases considerably. He is prone to giving more importance to success and fame than money. He has more enthusiasm or zest for life. If the ring finger is shorter than the index finger, it tends to reduce enthusiasm. If it is equal in length to the middle finger, a person's self-confidence increases beyond limits. He becomes interested in adventure and loves to take risks, like indulging in gambling, horse racing and speculation.

If the Mount of Mercury is prominent with a long ring finger, a person takes business risks. If he is in service, he tends to make money under the table by accepting bribes. If Aggressive Mars is also prominent, such a person makes a name for himself in sports competitions.

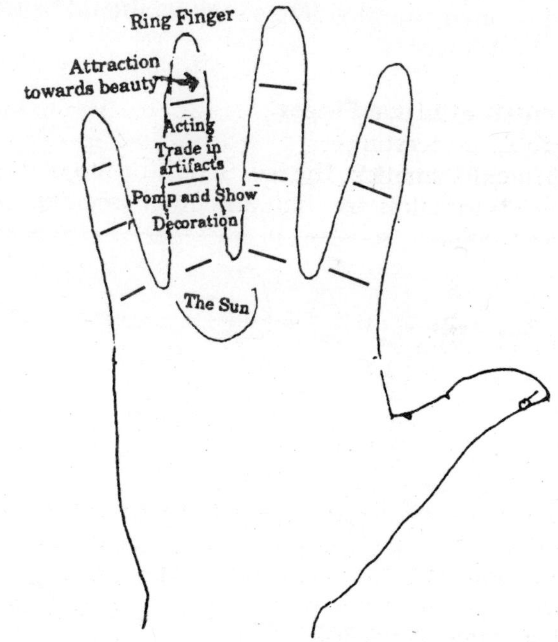

Fig. 7-C

A person with a short ring finger can never take a decision about anything, even if it involves a loss. If the first phalange is long, the person is attracted towards beauty. If the tip is rounded, he tends to love art. If the tip is spatulate in addition to the first phalange being long, the person loves to enjoy all beautiful things. He might have a vocation in which aesthetic appreciation is of essence. If such a phalange is accompanied by a square tip, the person is an idealist.

If the second phalange of the ring finger is long, the person is likely to be interested in acting/drama. He can gain from any trade connected with fine arts.

If the third phalange is long, the person is interested in pomp and show. If the third phalange is thick, the native will be devoid of artistic or creative ability. If the phalange is shaped like a waist, he would be interested in artistic activities.

If the setting of the ring finger is low, the person is devoid of any human sympathy. If it is high, it should be treated as a long third finger.

The Fourth or Little Finger

Though smallest in size, the fourth or little finger has greater importance in palmistry than any other (see Fig. 7-D).

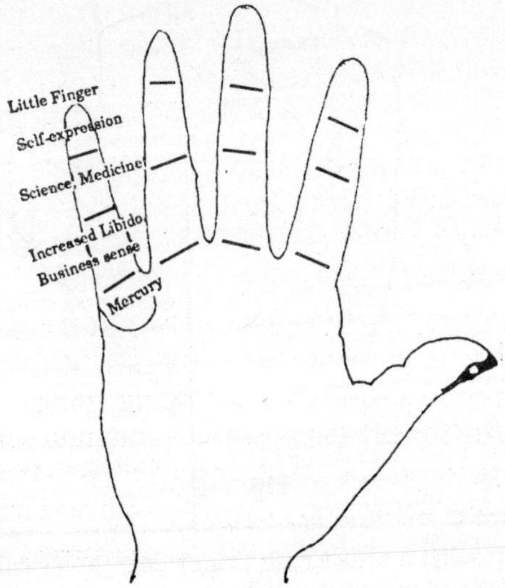

Fig. 7-D

The little finger represents the qualities of the planet Mercury. If it touches the first knot of the ring finger, it is considered to be of normal length. If it is a little below the first knot of the third finger, it is considered short; if a little above, it is longer than normal. Persons with a long little finger have the gift of the gab and are proficient in making and maintaining new contacts. Their nervous system is well-developed and they possess a sharp intelligence.

A long fourth finger helps a person to participate in politics, trade and every other sphere of human activity. Such a person knows how to make friends and to use them to his own advantage, but he is not interested in doing his duty towards his friends. Those with a small fourth finger suffer from an inferiority complex.

If the first phalange of the little finger is long, the person is proficient in expressing himself through art, but to have the gift of the gab, the little finger has to have a high setting. If the first phalange is long but the setting of the finger low, the person will not be eloquent, but can express himself through writing and other fine arts.

If the second phalange of the little finger is long, the person has proficiency in sciences, medicine and other branches of knowledge. Such persons are gainers in practical life.

If the third phalange is long, the person has a highly developed business/profession sense.

If the little finger is thick as the other fingers, the person is highly sexual. If along with this, there is a developed Aggressive Mars and a prominent Mount of Venus, the person does not bother about social mores so long as he can satisfy his sexual urge.

If the tip of the little finger is rounded, the person has a ready wit. If it is pointed, he is blessed with knowledge, cleverness and an artistic way of doing things. If the little finger is square, the person possesses common sense in great quantity. A person with a spatula-shaped tip to his little finger would have proficiency in civil engineering and other applied arts.

The little finger is generally in a low setting on the palm.

In such a case the person is prone to be taken in by glib talkers. He does not have the courage to stick to his guns. If the setting of the finger is high, the person tends to be arrogant.

Inclination of the Fingers

If the fingers, when spread out like a Japanese fan, are separate from each other and straight, it means that the peculiarities of the various mounts are in a balanced state.

If the fingers are inclined towards each other, it means that the finger which is inclined to another, passes on its energy to it.

If the first finger is inclined towards the thumb, the ego of the person is less in measure. If the index finger is inclined towards the middle one, it tends to reduce the seriousness and love for solitude of the individual. This is a special feature of the middle finger.

If the middle finger is inclined towards the index finger, it imparts its sobriety and intelligence to the first finger and reduces the degree of ego in the individual. If it inclines towards the third finger, its tendency to show off is reduced. Instead it creates a feeling of self-confidence in the individual. The person's tendency towards love for solitude is also less.

If the third finger is inclined towards the middle one, it imparts a bit of its extrovert nature to the latter and reduces its introvert tendencies. If it inclines towards the little finger, it reduces its tendency of selfishness and imparts a desire for fame instead.

If the little finger is inclined towards the third finger, it imparts its tendency towards selfishness and the ring finger's desire for fame is tinged with selfishness. The ring finger under the influence of an inclining little finger does not indicate desire for fame in its pure or idealistic form; the degree of idealism gets reduced. If the little finger is inclined outwards, away from the third finger, the person leads a careless life in which he does not bother about what he should do and the way in which it should be done.

If the fingers are inclined towards each other, but not

towards a particular point, the person suffers from indecisiveness of disposition. Such a person lacks firm resolve. If all the fingers are inclined towards the second or the Finger of Saturn, the peculiarities of Saturn tend to become prominent.

Spread of the Fingers

If the fingers, when spread, are inclined a little outwards, the person is able to adjust to every kind of environment. If they are inclined inwards, there is a tendency to stick to his position and be stubborn.

If the hand is so flexible that it can bend outwards like a plastic toy, it belongs to a person who cannot take any decision in life. Such persons are indecisive, artless and easily deceived. They are rumour-mongers also.

If the fingers are close together when extended straight outwards, but appear to overlap each other, and not in a straight line, they indicate a person who has no views of his own, nor does he stick to any opinion.

Distance Between the Fingers

If you spread your fingers like a Japanese fan, you will notice that the distance between them is not equal. The distance between the various fingers provides some clue about the inclinations of the person.

Normally the distance between two fingers in the middle (the middle and the ring finger) is the least as compared to others. If the distance is more, one should conclude that a person with such fingers tends to run away from family responsibilities. If the distances is less, the opposite is the case.

If the distance between the first and the second fingers is more than normal, the person is prone to justify his reasoning and is not susceptible to pressures. If it is less than normal, the converse is true.

If the gap between the ring finger and the little finger is more than normal, the person does not accept any ties. He has a strong will power and does exactly as he wishes. If the gap is narrow, the opposite is the case.

VIII

The Thumb

The thumb is the most important of all the digits which man has; without it, the fingers will not be able to grasp anything, nor would they have a point at which their tips could meet. It is the thumb which distinguishes man from other primates.

At the base of the thumb originates the Mount of Venus which indicates the degree of love, sympathy, sexuality and vital force a person possesses. But the thumb does not represent the qualities of Mount Venus; instead it represents that part of the brain which reveals the higher intelligence in a man. It is that intelligence which enables a person to distinguish between what is right and what is wrong.

A thumb which extends to the middle of the third phalange of the index finger is supposed to be of normal length. If it extends beyond, it is longer than normal and if it is short of the middle of the third phalange, it is considered shorter than normal. A thumb of a normal length indicates a normal development of the brain.

A short thumb indicates incomplete development of the brain. Persons with a short thumb act instinctively. Basic instincts like hunger and thirst, fear, sex, anger and jealousy move them sooner than others. If alongwith a short thumb, the Mount of Venus is well developed, it indicates that the person concerned would not give thought to what is improper so long as he can satisfy his sexual urge.

Persons with a longer-than-normal thumb are talented and crave for power. If alongwith the longer-than-normal thumb, they also have a longer-than-normal index finger accompanied by a well-developed Mount of Jupiter, they are likely to ascend to a position of power.

You must also study the head line when you find a long thumb in one of your clients. If the head line is not good, all the qualities associated with a long thumb turn into faults. We will deal with the head line in the related chapter.

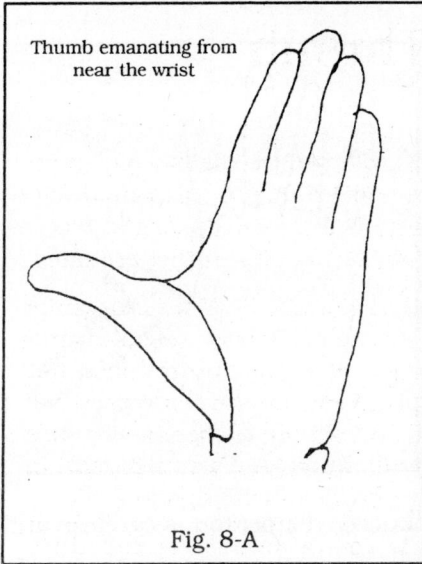

Thumb emanating from near the wrist

Fig. 8-A

A normal length of the thumb, is up to the middle of the third phalange of the index finger. We must also know the part of the palm from which the thumb originates. If it originates near the wrist the person is highly intelligent and has a fund of human sympathy (see Fig.8-A).

If the thumb originates from the Aggressive Mars (see Fig. 8-B), the person tries to fulfil his desires with physical force instead of his intelligence. If the Aggressive Mars is also prominent, the person is of quarrelsome nature,

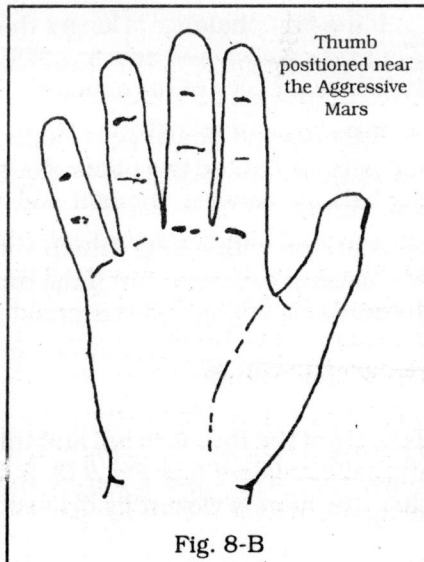

Thumb positioned near the Aggressive Mars

Fig. 8-B

If the thumb originating from near the Aggressive Mars extends to the middle of the third phalange of the index finger, the thumb would be considered short because it originates from a higher point.

Phalanges and Knots on the Thumbs

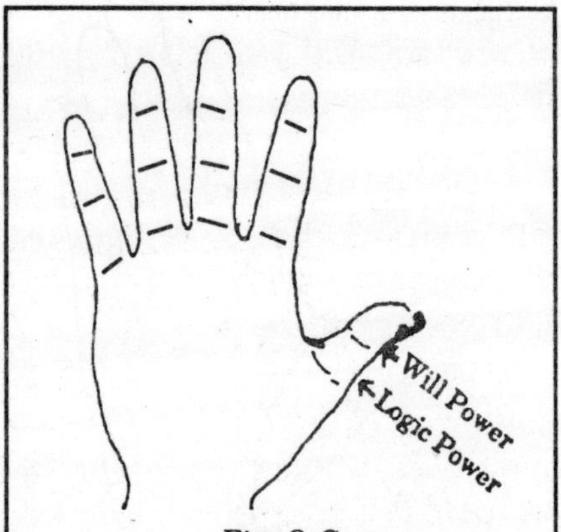

The thumb has only two phalanges — the first phalange is indicative of a person's will power and the second of his capacity for thought and analysis *(see Fig. 8-C)*. If the knot between the two phalanges is prominent, it indicates a cautios nature and the tendency to be wide awake. If the knot is soft or is not prominent enough to be noticed, the person is careless and lacks caution.

Fig. 8-C

If the first phalange is longer than the second, the person is of firm resolve, and acts in haste, without thinking about the consequences of his actions.

If the second phalange is longer, the person thinks more and acts less. If the two phalanges are equal in length, there is a balance between thought and action.

A person with a long thumb shows a firm resolve and is not harmful to others. But if the thumb is short and stubby, the person is selfish and concerned with personal needs only.

Tip of the Thumb

If the tip of the thumb is full and thick, the person is zealous and self-confident *(see Fig. 8-D)*. If the first phalange is like a club, the man is violent by disposition *(see Fig. 8-E)*.

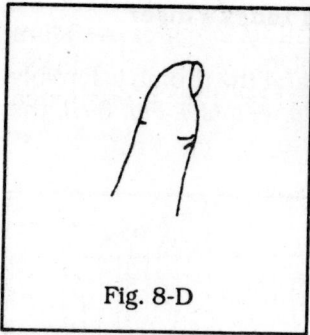

Fig. 8-D

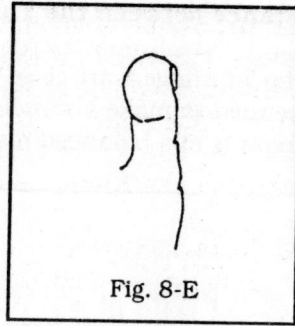

Fig. 8-E

If the tip is flat like the end of an oar, the person is stubborn. If the tip is square, he is likely to have administrative ability. If the tip is conic, the person cannot make any resolutions.

If the second phalange of the thumb is narrow in the middle, it is called a waist-like thumb. A person with such a thumb does not have the courage to express his views openly. But there is a finesse in his actions. If the second phalange is thick, the person is fearless but clumsy in his actions.

Inclination of the Thumb

If the thumb inclines inward when extended, the person is likely to be of a violent disposition.

If the inclination is outwards *(see Fig. 8-F)* the person dislikes violence. If the thumb is straight, the person has a balanced disposition and a strong quality of resoluteness *(see Fig. 8-G)*.

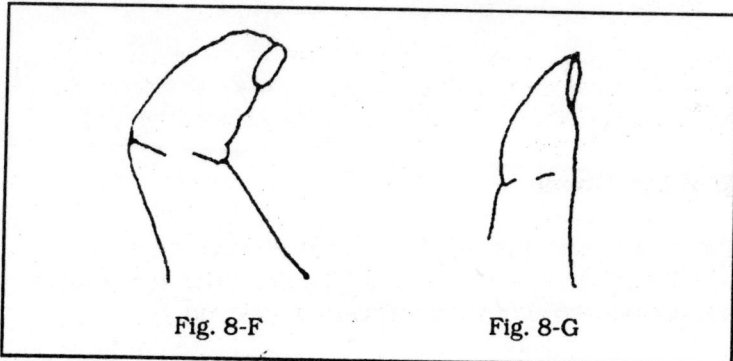

Fig. 8-F

Fig. 8-G

Distance between the Thumb and Index Finger

If the four fingers are close together and the thumb is forcibly extended to make an angle of 90 degrees (*see Fig. 8-H*), the person is of a balanced disposition.

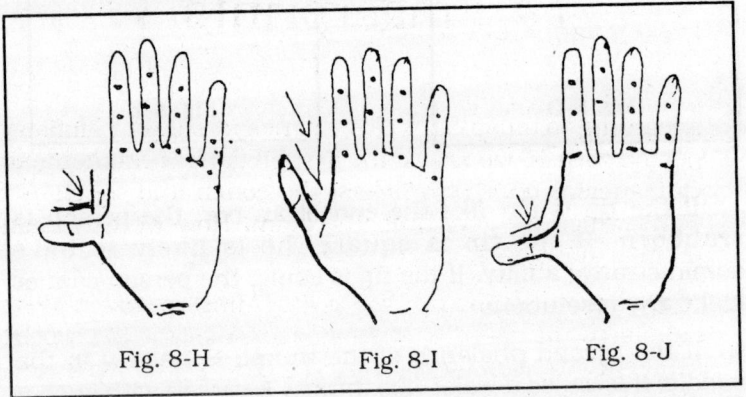

Fig. 8-H   Fig. 8-I   Fig. 8-J

But if the angle is less than 90 degrees (*see Fig. 8-I*), there is less of balance and less capacity to adjust to his surroundings. The narrower the angle, the greater is the love for conventions and traditions.

If the angle is obtuse (i.e. more than 90 degrees) (*see Fig. 8-J*) the person is wayward and does not care to take advice from others.

IX
Fingerprints

According to a popular belief in ancient Hindu palmistry, a person with 10 whorls on the first phalange becomes a king. Our ancient texts also talk of the conch and shell — the signs which are found on the palm. How we can identify them is still a matter of conjecture.

Not much importance was given to fingerprints in western palmistry till about a century ago. Most of the work on fingerprints has been done by the police and crime investigation agencies. The results of their research were so impressive that palmists thought it fit to make them a part of their repertory.

Most palmists attach importance to the lines of the palm, but the fingerprints are no less important. On examining them, you can tell a lot about the health and mentality of the person. It becomes easier to read a person's fate if the fingerprints are examined alongwith the lines of the palm.

The designs on the fingerprints are slightly different from each other, but the fingerprints have been divided by experts into six patterns or designs. All the patterns are given in *Fig. 9-A to 9-F.*

Fingerprints are easy to reproduce on a paper with a smooth surface. Just press your finger ends on the surface of the stamp inking-pad and take the prints on the paper, just as an illiterate person affixes his thumb impression on legal documents. It is better to clean the fingertips before taking prints. The fingerprints should be visible to the naked eye, but, if they are not, use a magnifying lens to study them.

Samples of fingerprints are given together with their drawings for greater clarity. Let us now see what the various patterns stand for.

Whorl

A whorl normally indicates how resolute a person is. If there are whorls on the fingers, the man is stubborn and does not change his views. Such a person needs mental relaxation because he stays under continuous stress and tension which are his way of life, making him susceptible to heart ailments (see Fig. 9-A).

Fig. 9-A

Arch

An arch indicates of outward peace but an inner turmoil. If a person with an arch is placed in an environment which does not suit him, he is likely to lose his balance of mind. Such persons are suspicious by nature. If somebody is kind enough to listen to their problems, they feel drained of their worries and are at peace with themselves. A person with too many arches is liable to face disorders of the digestive system (see Fig. 9-B).

Fig. 9-B

Tented Arch

Tented arches are found but rarely.
Being less tolerant, such persons are
always under some kind of tension.
They are likely to fall prey to nervous
disorders *(see Fig. 9-C)*.

Fig. 9-C

Loop

A loop is common to most palms. Such
persons have the ability to adjust to
all kinds of circumstances. They do
not stick to any view for long. However,
they have a weak digestive system *(see
Fig. 9-D)*.

Fig. 9-D

Closed Loop

A closed loop is also known as a
peacock's eye. Persons with this
pattern on their fingers are moderates
— they have neither the stubbornness
of a whorl, nor the flexibility of a loop
(see Fig. 9-E).

Fig. 9-E

Composite Loop/Double Loop

Vacillation is the hallmark of a person with a double loop and it is not easy for him to take a decision. He does not easily trust anybody and is generally subject to nervous tension (see Fig. 9-F).

Fig. 9-F

A Mixed Pattern

Very few individuals have similar patterns on all the 10 digits. If there is a mixed pattern, the nature of the person is determined by the preponderance of the pattern on the fingers. If the person does not have the same pattern, then you should give double weightage to the pattern on the thumbs.

X
Fingernails

Fingernails are the windows which open into a man's inner mind. They tell an observer a lot about the man's health, his vital force and his disposition.

The fingertips are extremely sensitive, because they contain bunches of nerve ends. The nails act as a protective cover for them.

The colour, size, shape and shine of the nails is determined by the amount of hormones and the level of blood present in the body. Trace elements (minerals) in the body also influence the shape and size of the nails. If all the elements, including the hormones, are in a state of balance in the body, it takes about five months for the nail to grow. The time may be shorter or longer, depending on the age or the amount of hormones present in the body.

The nail starts growing from its base, and can tell us when an abnormality first appears in a nail. In other words, if there is a whitish spot at the base of the nail or a horizontal ridge at the base of the finger, it might be of recent origin, say about a month. If it is towards the fingertip, it might have started about four months ago.

An Ideal Nail

An ideal nail is one which is pinkish in colour, has a healthy shine, is sufficiently long as well as broad, and bulges outward, slightly like a TV screen. Such a nail indicates good mental as well as physical health.

We now come to the characteristics of the different kinds of nails.

Colour of the Nails

Pinkish nails indicate a fine state of health and a liberal disposition.

Red nails are a sign of excessive physical energy, anger and a tendency towards violence.

White nails are associated with egotism and a rash nature.

A yellow nail indicates disorders of the liver, usually jaundice.

Blue nails indicate lack of oxygen in the body and excess of carbon dioxide. Women generally have a blue tinge to their nails at the time they start menstruating and also at menopause. At other periods in their lives, blue nails are an indication of ill health and persons with such nails should be advised to consult a physician. Blueness at the base of the nail indicates a heart ailment which is easy to cure.

A blackish tinge in the nails indicates diseased blood. Being physically weak, such persons are liable to be irritable and fall prey to every possible sickness.

Whatever be the colour of the nail, if it maintains its shine, there is not much cause for alarm.

Size and Shape of Nails

Large nail: A nail which is long as well as broad indicates a placid temperament and tact in dealing with others. If such a nail has a shine, the person possesses good physical and mental health (*see Fig. 10-A*).

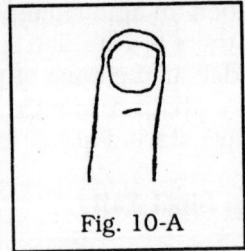

Fig. 10-A

Small nail: A small nail is broad enough to cover the whole breadth of the finger, but is not long enough. Such a person is not tolerant and is quick to think that what he has decided is for the best. It is fruitless to argue with such a person. He is likely to fall prey to nervous and cardiac disorders (*see Fig. 10-B*).

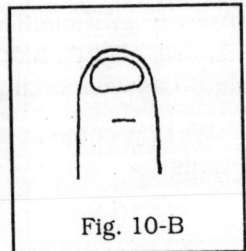

Fig. 10-B

All the Secrets of Palmistry

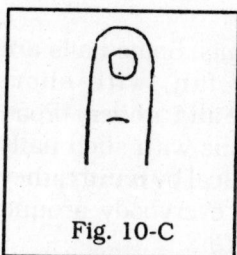

Fig. 10-C

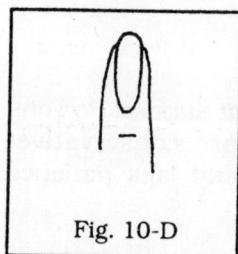

Fig. 10-D

Very small nail: Such a nail is short in both length and breadth and appears like a spot at the end of the finger. Persons with such a nail are likely to make fun of others and are thrifty by nature *(see Fig. 10-C).*

Long Nail: A long nail is one which is of a very short breadth. If you look at it from a distance, it seems to carry a vertical line. Those with a long nail are close-mouthed plotters. Artistic by nature, they do not have it within them to give expression to their ability and are thus a frustrated lot. They have a strong nervous system but limited physical energy *(see Fig. 10-D).*

Study the Shape in Addition to Size

Study of the shape of the nail in addition to its size are important. The following are the most common shapes of nails found in human beings:

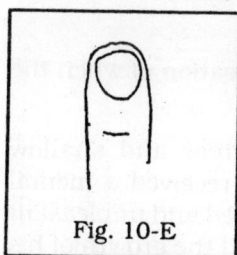

Fig. 10-E

Round nails: Nails which appear rounded both at the base and the ends are called round nails. A person with such nails is healthy, active and has a friendly disposition. He bears his responsibilities towards his family seriously *(see Fig. 10-E).*

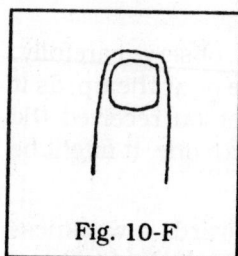

Fig. 10-F

Square nails: Both at the base and the ends of the nails appear to be square. Persons with square nails are methodical and calculating by nature *(see Fig. 10-F).*

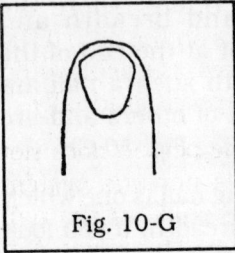

Fig. 10-G

Fan-shaped nails: Some nails are like a Japanese fan, with short breadth at the base and are very broad at the ends. Persons with such nails are moody and critical by nature, they are suspicious of everybody around them *(see Fig. 10-G).*

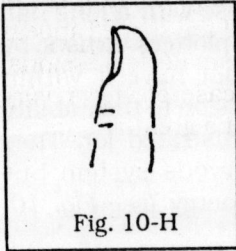

Fig. 10-H

Nails with a flat surface: Persons with such nails are conservative, easily frustrated and lack patience *(see Fig. 10-H).*

Spots on the nails: White spots on the nails indicate nervousness and mental tension. If a person with such nails reduces the mental work that he/she does and remains away from excitement and tension, they can be easily handled.

Blackish and yellowish spots indicate failures in life and ill health.

The position of spots can give an indication of when the disorder could have begun first.

Stripes on the nails: Horizontal stripes and shallow depressions indicate that a person has received a mental shock. It show that because of an unwanted and unpleasant situation, the person faced in life, affected the growth of his nails. Such a person should regularly get his heart rate and blood pressure checked.

If there is only one stripe or depression, observe carefully, if it is at the base of the nail, in the middle or at the tip, as it can give a clue to the time when the person received the shock. If the number of stripes is more than one, it might be an indication of a series of shocks.

Vertical stripes: Such stripes point towards a weakness in the nervous system. The cause might be lack of mineral trace elements which are vital for the brain. Before the appearance of such stripes, a spot appears on the nail. If the person concerned takes remedial measures, the spot would move towards the tip of the nail and disappear gradually.

If after noticing the spot on a nail the person does not become careful and the pressure on his nervous system continues, stripes start forming and the shine of the nail disappears. The number of stripes indicate the amount of stress that the person is subject to. The more the number of stripes, the greater the amount of stress. If the stripes appear on a large nail on which there are also small depressions, then they are not harmful, but in the case of either very short or very long nails, they indicate that a great amount of harm has been caused to the individual.

XI

Signs on the Palm

The following two kinds of signs are found on the palm:

Chance Lines or Lines of Influence would be frequently referred to and should be dealt with at the earliest. Chance Lines are those which have not yet been named. We would go into their details along with the main and secondary lines at the appropriate places in the next few chapters.

Frequent references are found in the *Samudrika Shastra* to signs found on the palm, like the chariot, mount, umbrella, flag, tree, temple, water pitcher, lotus, bow, sword, plough, lion, elephant, etc. These signs are hardly found in the shapes in which they are represented in the pictures or figures.

According to modern palmistry, we can easily recognise the signs on the palms. They are a cross, star, square, spot, triangle, island, grill, tassel, trident, etc. We will discuss the influence these signs exercise on a person's fate at appropriate places. Presently it would suffice to say that it is best to identify the methods as also the main points about their suitability or otherwise.

Cross: If two Chance Lines cross each other, a cross is formed *(see Fig. 11-A)*. If the cross is on the Mount of Jupiter, it is auspicious but becomes inauspicious if found

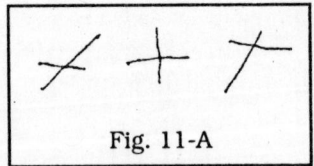

Fig. 11-A

at other places. If it is found on the Mount of Venus and the Mount of Sun, the effect might be good or bad when taken in conjunction with other characteristics of the hand.

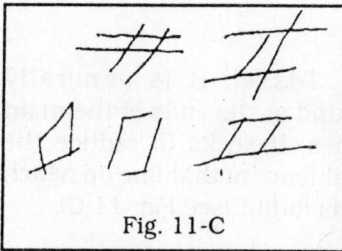

Fig. 11-B

Star: If more than two Lines of Influence intersect each other, a star is formed *(see Fig. 11-B)*. If the star is on the Mount of Jupiter, it is a positive sign. If its location is on the other mounts, like those of Venus, Apollo (Sun) or Mercury, then it can be positive or negative, depending on the other characteristics of the hand.

Square: If four lines intersect each other in such a way so as to form a rectangular shape, it is called a square *(see Fig. 11-C)*. If a square is found on any mount or any line, it indicates that all obstacles caused by that mount or line would be removed.

Fig. 11-C

Spot: A piece of skin on the palm which has a darker shade is called a spot. Some palmists call a small round depression as a spot. There are differences in opinion about their effects but it is bad sign.

Triangle: A triangle, as the very name suggests, is formed when three lines come from three directions. It is good wherever it is found *(see Fig. 11-D)*.

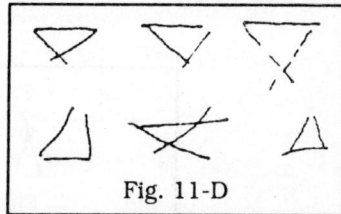

Fig. 11-D

Island: When a line splits to join further on and forms an oval shape, it is called an island. Its influence is bad no matter where it is found *(see Fig. 11-E)*.

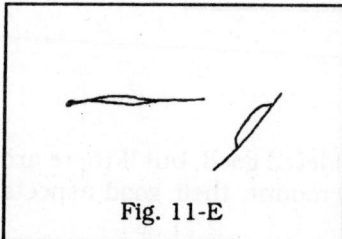

Fig. 11-E

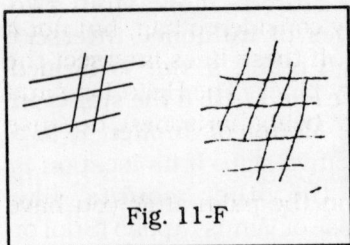

Fig. 11-F

Grill: If three or more vertical lines are crossed or intersected by three other or more horizontal lines, a grill is formed. The sign is generally bad. In some cases, when it is found on the Mount of Venus, it might prove good. I will go into futher details when we come to the Mount of Venus *(see Fig. 11-F).*

Fig. 11-G

Tassel: It is generally found at the ends of the main lines. It seeks to reduce the influence of that line on which it is found *(see Fig. 11-G).*

Trident: If a trident is found at the end of a vertical line and its three ends are vertical. It indicates a general development of the line and the mount which is situated at its base. If it is at the end of a horizontal line or a circular line, its influence is according to the strength of that line *(see Fig. 11-H).*

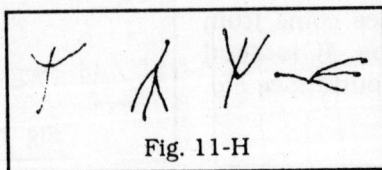

Fig. 11-H

Other Aspects

Vertical lines are generally considered good, but if there are more than two such lines on a mount, their good aspects are weakened.

Horizontal lines are generally considered bad, but not if they are on the Mount of Venus. If these lines intersect the main lines, they are called Worry Lines. The Head Line and Heart Line are not bad in spite of being horizontal, because that is their natural position.

Try to identify these signs on the palm after you have studied the next chapter.

XII
Mounts on the Palm (A)

We have given a broad outline on the various mounts on the palm in an earlier chapter. We will discuss the details of the mounts here.

The mounts are better indicators of a person's disposition, health and inclination than the lines are, one cannot interpret the lines without a proper study of the mounts. For example, if a person wants advice about what business he should engage in, or the type of employment he should seek, or

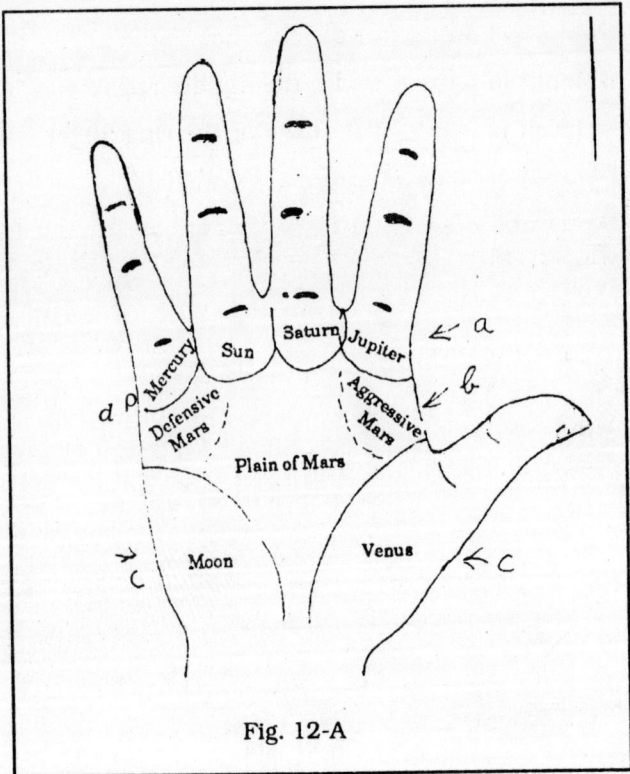

Fig. 12-A

All the Secrets of Palmistry

what disease in particular he is susceptible to, you would have to study his mounts along with the lines before coming to any conclusion.

Let me repeat here, there are no shortcuts to acquiring knowledge of palmistry. One has to study it with patience before one gets a modicum of knowledge to answer all the queries.

The mounts on the palm can be divided into three parts *(see Fig. 12-A)*:

1. Mounts at the base of the fingers *(see Fig. 12-Aa)*.

2. Mounts in the middle *(see Fig. 12-Ab)*.

3. Mounts near the wrist *(see Fig 12-Ac)*.

There are four mounts at the base of the fingers *(see Fig. 12-B)*.

a. Mount of Jupiter under the Index finger

b. Mount of Saturn under the middle finger

c. Mount of Apollo or Sun under the ring finger

d. Mount of Mercury under the little finger

If you want to locate the mounts at the base of the fingers, look for the ridge pattern on the skin which is in the shape of the letter Y. The arrow marks—a,b,c and d are given in *Fig. 12-B*.

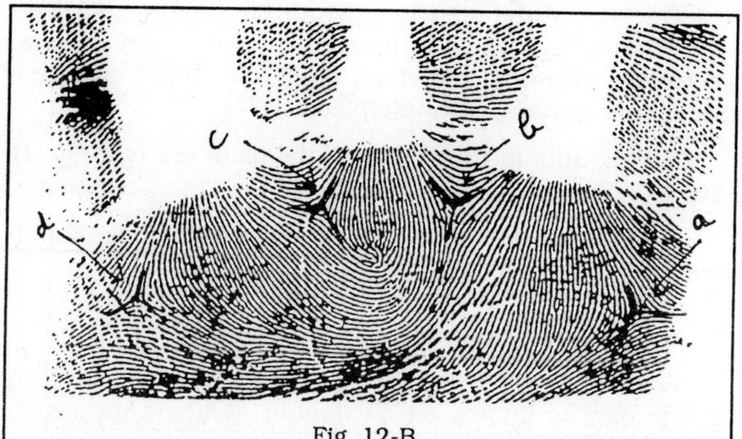

Fig. 12-B

The skin ridge pattern is easily visible on a hard and rough skin, but if the hand is flexible, soft or flabby, you have to strain your eyes to discern it. It is called the apex of the mount. If the site of the apex is prominent, i.e. slightly protruding, the mount is considered developed. If, in addition to being developed, it is hard too, it is called overdeveloped. If there is no bulge at the mount, it is underdeveloped. If there is a depression at the site of the mount, it is known as a deficit. If the mount is not raised but there are raised portions around its site, it is known as a displaced mount.

If there is no bulge at the site of the mount, but a vertical line is seen, it should be read as a developed mount. But if the mount is raised and there is no vertical line over it, its special features tend to get diminished. If there are two vertical lines over the mount, it should be treated as an over-developed mount.

Too many vertical lines tend to destroy the influence of the mount, but such lines on the Mount of Mercury indicate a tendency towards ability to carry out research.

Horizontal lines on the mount produce a bad effect.

In the chapter on fingers we stated that if a finger is long or is in a high setting on the palm, it tends to accentuate the qualities of the mount. Converse is the case when the finger is short or is in a low setting on the palm. One must, therefore, study the length of the finger and its setting while reading the effect of the mount.

The sign of the apex is only on the mounts concerned with the various fingers; there is no such sign on other mounts. One must, therefore, study the raised surface of the mount at its appropriate place.

The mounts in the middle of the palm are *(see Fig. 12-Ab)*:

1. Defensive or Negative Mars (also called Upper Mars)

2. Aggressive or Positive or Lower Mars

3. The Plain of Mars

Some palmists divide the Plain of Mars in two parts: the upper part is known as *Ketusthan*. It lies between the

All the Secrets of Palmistry

Aggressive and the Defensive Mars. The lower part lies between the Mount of Venus and the Mount of Moon and is called the *Rahusthan* or the Mount of Neptune. But most palmists describe it as the Plain of Mars. It would be better to stick to this nomenclature if one is to give a proper reading of the effect of this Plain of Mars.

There are two mounts near the wrist *(see Fig. 12-Ac):*

1. The Mount of Luna or the Moon

2. The Mount of Venus

We will go into the details of the mounts as they seem on the palm. The following is based on research in western palmistry. References are made to *Samudrika Shastra* of ancient India, where necessary. The cold and hot effects of the various mounts are also discussed in the following paragraphs.

Mounts at the Base of the Fingers

Mount of Jupiter

The Mount of Jupiter lies at the base of the first or the index finger. According to the treatise on Hindu palmistry *Samudrika Shastra* of ancient India, it is called the *Pitristhan* (the place of ancestors). It is supposed to have a hot effect *(see Fig. 12-B-1).*

Three main lines, viz. the Heart Line, the Head Line and the Life Line originate near the Mount of Jupiter. Benham gives special importance to the index finger which is supposed to represent this mount.

The Mount of Jupiter indicates the characteristics of leadership, egotism, ambition and the desire for respect. Persons with a prominent Mount of Jupiter are religious and devoted to conventions and traditions. They follow certain ideals. Even if such persons engage in some dishonourable profession, they follow a certain code of conduct.

The setting of the index finger decides the influence of this mount. If the index finger is in a low setting, the effect

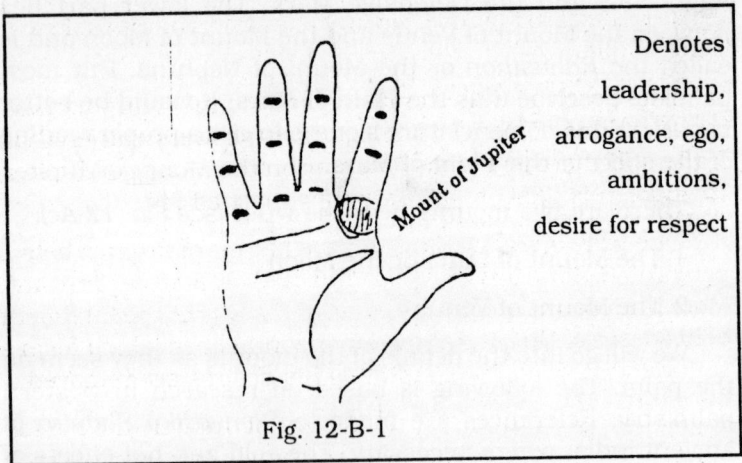

Denotes leadership, arrogance, ego, ambitions, desire for respect

Mount of Jupiter

Fig. 12-B-1

of the mount is reduced. Conversely, if the setting of this finger is high, the effect of the Mount of Jupiter is enhanced. The length of the index finger also affects the influence of this mount. We have given the effect of the high and low setting of the fingers in Chapter VI.

If the index finger is longer than the ring finger, it tends to heighten the effect of the Mount of Jupiter. If the index finger is set high and the Mount of Jupiter is developed, the person is dominated by this mount.

A developed or underdeveloped mount affects the influence of the Mount of Jupiter. If the Mount of Saturn is developed or the middle finger is extra long, the ego of the person is restricted. If the Mount of the Sun is also developed, the person becomes a leader. If the Mount of Mercury is equally well developed, the qualities of idealism in a person are restricted, but the desire for leadership or a position of power is high.

If the Defensive Mars is well developed, there is a desire for leadership and the tendency towards hasty decisions is reduced. If the Aggressive Mars is helpful, the person might become fit to lead the police, the armed forces or sports teams. With a favourable Mount of Venus, a person has a happy disposition and he gets what he wants. With a developed Mount of Moon, a person desires to be the best in the field of arts.

All the Secrets of Palmistry

If the Mount of Jupiter is overdeveloped, the person's ego turns into arrogance. He loves flatterers and people who cling to him.

Those with a levelled or depressed Mount of Jupiter have no ambitions. They tend to become followers rather than leaders. If there is a cross or a star on the Mount of Jupiter, the person is likely to lead a happy married life.

One or two vertical lines on the Mount of Jupiter help a person to fulfil his wishes. Such a person is never in want. More than two vertical lines come in the way of the fulfilment of his desires. But, if there are horizontal lines which form a square, the obstacles to fulfilling his desires are removed.

If there is a square on the Mount of Jupiter, the person has administrative ability. With a triangle present, a person shows political sagacity. With a grill over the Mount of Jupiter, the person thinks of big things. An island spoils his future.

A person with a prominent Mount of Jupiter is fond of eating and drinking and remains healthy. Because of the hot effect of the planet, there might be a possibility of high blood pressure, carelessness in eating a proper diet might lead to diseases of the digestive tract in such a person. But if he is careful about what he eats and drinks and is able to control his ego by reading good literature, there is little likelihood of his suffering from any disease.

Mount of Saturn

This mount is found at the base of the second or the middle finger. According to the treatise on Hindu palmistry, *Samudrika Shastra*, the mount is known as *Matristhan* (place of the mother). According to research by the author, its effect is cold *(see Fig. 12-C)*.

The Mount of Saturn is not generally found in a developed state. It is, on the other hand, slightly depressed. In spite of this, each individual has some qualities of this mount because the middle finger is generally in a high setting and its length is also greater than that of the other fingers. If alongwith this, you find a more developed Saturn, it should be taken

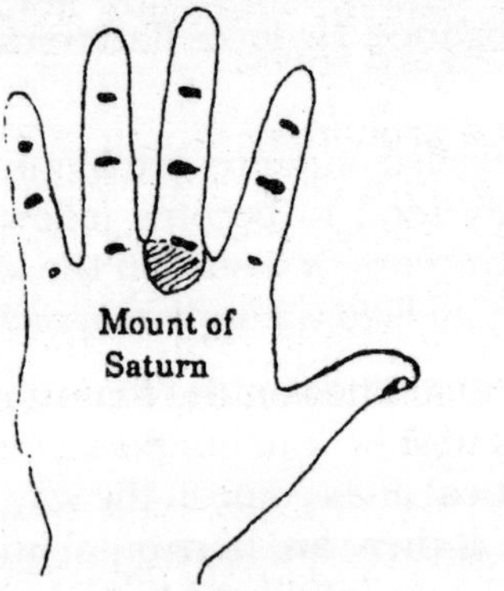

Sobriety, sagacity, stability, love for solitude, capacity for planning

Mount of Saturn

Fig. 12-C

to be overdeveloped. If the middle and the ring fingers are of equal length, the Mount of Saturn should be considered underdeveloped. If the setting of the finger is low, it should be taken as a depressed mount. In short, the middle finger is usually higher than the other fingers and so the Mount of Saturn is considered to be developed.

If the middle finger is longer than usual, its setting is high and there are one or two vertical lines over the Mount of Saturn. Such a person should be considered to be strongly influenced by this planet.

The Mount of Saturn is indicative of a person's sobriety, steadfastness and sagacity. Such a person is generally an introvert. You will not find him laughing nor weeping even when the occasion demands it. He tends to smile when happy but hides his sorrow from others.

Persons with a predominant Mount of Saturn do not like to mix with others and, hence, make few friends. But once they call a person their friend, they stand by him through thick and thin. They love solitude and are fond of reading and writing. They are good planners and their favourite pastime is research. They analyse things as a matter of habit. The field of their plans and research depends on the other signs on their palm. Planning, plotting and finding fault, for example, stem from the same basic cause — the habit of analysing things. A short thumb with a rough skin helps to reduce the effect of Saturn, whereas a long thumb and a flexible skin produce good effects.

If a person with a prominent Mount of Saturn works in an office, he tends to love desk-work. Public relations is a difficult chore for him. He marries out of need and not out of love. Such a person is laconic in speech and able to keep secrets. Because of a stable temperament, he joins a profession or trade where he is able to continue working for long without any change.

A long palm and long fingers tend to accentuate the qualities of Saturn, whereas a broad palm reduces its effect.

Persons with a predominant Mount of Saturn are thrifty by nature and never take any risk in financial matters. They are interested in avenues where the profits are certain and where bodily strength is of little importance. They are found engaged in real estate transactions and money-lending.

It the Mount of Saturn is flanked by Jupiter on one side and Mount of Apollo or Sun on the other, both exercise a hot effect. If these two mounts are developed, their heat and cold normally associated with Saturn, get reduced. This means lack of love for solitude and sobriety of disposition. One must, therefore, see the position in which these two mounts are before reading the effect of Saturn.

If, in addition to a developed Mount of Saturn, a person has a developed Mount of Moon, he is likely to be gloomy, suspicious, irritable and miserly by nature. If his Mount of Mercury is developed, then he indulges in illegal activities. If, at the same time, the Defensive Mars is well developed, he thinks deeply and has patience. Aggressive Mars and the Mount of Venus are generally under-developed in a hand with a prominent Mount of Saturn. But, if they are well developed, they are likely to impart their vigour and reduce the features peculiar to Saturn.

If the finger on the Mount of Saturn is short or has a low setting, the person is not sober but clumsy.

A single vertical line on Saturn increases a person's good fortune. If there are two such lines, it takes long for the person to realise his dreams of achieving prosperity. More than two vertical lines or a grill make his brain more active. Too much of such a situation is bad.

Palmists of the old era considered the presence of a cross or star on the Mount of Saturn as indicative of a person going to prison or meeting with an accident. But the new breed of palmists are of the view that it is just an indication of ill luck. If there is a square, the person might escape misfortune. A triangle indicates interest in the occult sciences and horizontal lines show failure in experiments.

Persons with a developed Mount of Saturn have, generally speaking, a long life, but there is danger of their suffering from minor disorders of the bones, flatulence and digestion. Carelessness can convert minor ailments into serious disorders; for example, flatulence might degenerate into diseases like gout, rheumatism and may even bad to paralysis.

Mount of Apollo or Sun

This mount is situated at the base of the ring finger. According to the, *Samudrika Shastra*, this is the *Vidyasthan* or the place of learning. According to the author's research, it has a hot effect *(see Fig. 12-D)*.

This mount indicates the desire of an individual to acquire prominence. It also signifies hope, zeal, enthusiasm, liberalism and desire for fame.

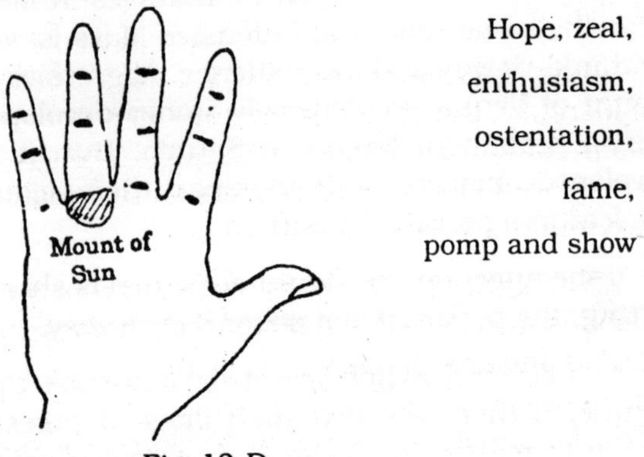

Hope, zeal,
enthusiasm,
ostentation,
fame,
pomp and show

Mount of Sun

Fig. 12-D

All the Secrets of Palmistry

Generally this mount is not developed. Vertical lines on this mount show that the mount is developed. If the ring finger is longer than the first or the index finger, the person is predominantly under the influence of the Sun.

Like a person with a prominent Mount of Jupiter, a prominent Mount of Sun ensures that the person will not take to evil ways. Even if such a person takes to some dishonourable act, he maintains a certain code of conduct.

A person with a prominent Mount of Jupiter is ambitious, but his ambitions are fulfilled only if the Mount of Sun is also developed. Those with a prominent Mount of Sun have a happy disposition. They are open minded and do not hide things. They are interested in the arts, but also have desire for the good things of life.

Persons with an overdeveloped Mount of Sun have a longing for ostentation. Their desires are so many that there is no chance of their getting fulfilled. Because they expect too much, their married life is miserable and their friends are liable to ditch them.

If along with a developed Mount of Sun, the third finger is longer than the first, there is an increased tendency to take risks. Such persons are likely to engage in trades which witness frequent fluctuations.

A person with an underdeveloped Mount of Sun (without vertical lines) has no desire for show. He is satisfied if he gets two meals a day, a few clothes on his back and a place to live in.

If a displaced Mount of Sun inclines towards the Mount of Mercury, the person is pragmatic. Inclination towards the Mount of Saturn brings sobriety in his disposition. In short, a displaced Mount of Sun takes on the qualities of the other two mounts adjacent to it.

If in addition to a prominent Mount of Sun, the Mount of Moon is also developed, a person becomes successful in the field of fine arts. If the Mount of Mercury is strong, the desire for fame is fulfilled and the person gains monetary benefits. If the Mount of Saturn is also developed the tendency towards showing off gets reduced. With a developed Defensive Mars, the desire to take hasty decisions is checked. An Aggressive Mars ensures success in endeavours in which physical labour is required. If the Mount of Venus is also developed, a person's sexual desires tend to be fulfilled.

One or two vertical lines on the Mount of Sun take a person towards progress, whereas more than two lines ensure belated success.

If there is a cross on the Mount of Sun, the person has to struggle to get recognition. A star brings good luck but there is danger of suffering from eye ailments.

Horizontal lines on the Mount of Sun signify impediments to success. There might be vanity and pretension in the person as a result of this. A triangle on the mount ensures success in the field of science. A square protects a person against the consequences of haste and lack of self-control.

A person with a prominent Mount of Sun generally remains healthy, but because of the hot effect of the planet, he is prone to fall prey to disorders of the heart, the eye and blood. But, by exercising care, the person can avoid these disorders.

Mount of Mercury

The Mount of Mercury is situated at the base of the fourth or little finger. According to the *Samudrika Shastra*, this is the place of achievement, or *Jayasthan*. The author's research in this matter led him to believe that in addition to its hot effect, there is something of the cold also in this mount. That is why the total effect is less hot *(see Fig. 12-E)*.

This mount indicates a desire to take advantage of one's own common sense, business acumen, gift of the gab and the capacity for research.

If the little finger is longer than normal and its setting is high, and the mount is well developed, the person is credited with a prominent Mount of Mercury.

Such a person is an optimist, desires change, is talented and dynamic. When confronted with an opportunity to gain something, he does not bother about social conventions. Such

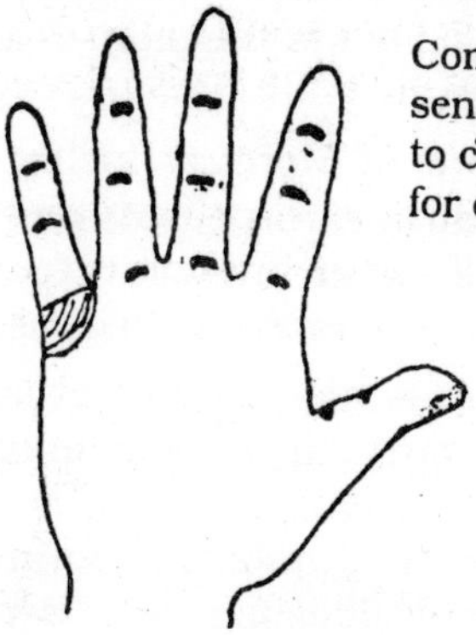

Common sense, business sense, gift of the gab, wish to conduct research, desire for change, dynamism

Fig. 12-E

a person is fit to undertake work related to public relations.

The person is not of stable disposition and desires change and movement from place to place. It is in his nature to do everything quickly and that is why he always lacks mental peace.

Persons with a prominent Mount of Mercury understand the character of the person they are dealing with and are able to adjust themselves to the needs of the hour. Whether in trade or service, they are able to advance their interests.

These people are not strong physically, but their intellect is sharp. They understand things and are quick to decide. That is why they generally succeed in their designs.

Persons with an overdeveloped Mount of Mercury are liars and cheats. If the little finger is crooked, it enhances this quality.

A person with an underdeveloped Mount of Mercury is innocent and without any guile. He does not have the gift of the gab. If such a person takes to business, he is liable to suffer losses as compared to persons with a prominent Mount of Mercury.

If the signs on the palm of a person with a prominent Mount of Mercury are favourable, then he will take to a honourable profession or vocation. If the signs are bad, he will take to committing a crime. One must, therefore, look for these signs before one reads the palm of a person with a prominent Mount of Mercury.

If a displaced Mount of Mercury inclines towards the Mount of Apollo or Sun, the person earns fame as a researcher in science. If the inclination is towards the outer edge of the palm, it tends to increase his business acumen.

If the Mount of Sun is also developed in addition to a developed Mount of Mercury, the person tends to earn fame. If the Mount of Saturn is developed, he is likely to hatch conspiracies. The Mount of Jupiter in conjunction with the Mount of Mercury impart idealism to a person's life. The Defensive Mars tends to reduce uneasiness and the person develops a stable temperament. The Mount of Moon contributes to uneasiness and a desire for travel. With the help of a developed Mount of Venus, the tendency to indulge in sexual relations that are frowned upon by the society is increased. An Aggressive Mars is rarely to be seen in conjunction with a developed Mount of Mercury, but if it is so, then it tends to increase the desire to ignore social mores in preference to sexual needs.

A prominent Mount of Mercury and a longer than normal little finger is the hallmark of successful politicians, public speakers, businessmen and researchers.

A single vertical line on the Mount of Mercury indicates the possibility of acquiring sudden wealth. More of such lines indicate interest in research. Many vertical lines on the Mount of Mercury in the palms of a scientist or doctor tend to add to his ability.

If there is a grill over the Mount of Mercury, it indicates a tendency towards cheating others. Horizontal lines coming from the edge (percussion) of the palm over the Mount of Mercury indicate the possibility of marriage or the degree of sexuality present. A triangle indicates political acumen and a spot is indicative of losses in business. A square saves a person from monetary loss and also from competition.

A person with a prominent Mount of Mercury is more prone to nervous disorders. He is also susceptible to disorders of the digestive system. But, if the person takes care, he can save himself from these troubles.

All the Secrets of Palmistry

XIII
Mounts on the Palm (B)

Mounts or Areas in the Middle of the Palm

The planet Mars is associated with courage, bravery and fortitude. Western palmists have designated the area between the Mount of Mercury and the Mount of Moon as the Upper Mars *(see Fig. 13-A)*, because generally the area lies above the Head Line. We call it the Defensive Mars because of its peculiarities.

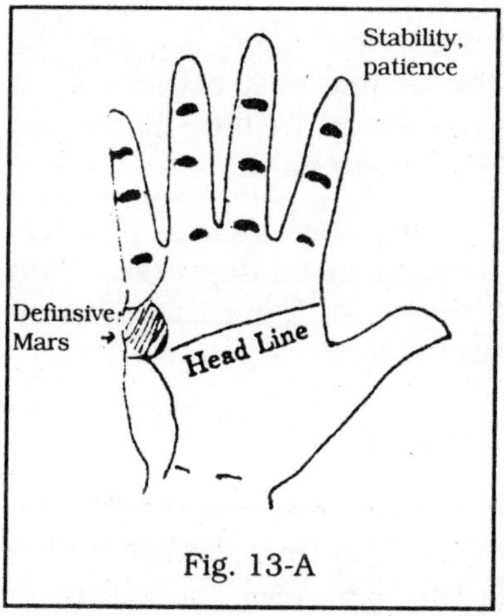

Fig. 13-A

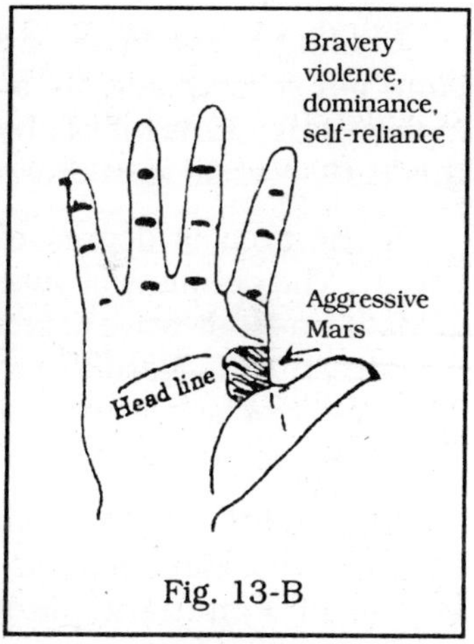

Fig. 13-B

Western palmists have designated the area between the Mount of Jupiter and Venus as the Lower Mars *(see Fig. 13-B)*, because it lies generally below the Head Line. We call it the Aggressive Mars because of its characteristics.

The area lying between these two Mars and the mounts of Venus and Luna has been designated as the Plain of Mars by western palmists *(see Fig. 13-C)*.

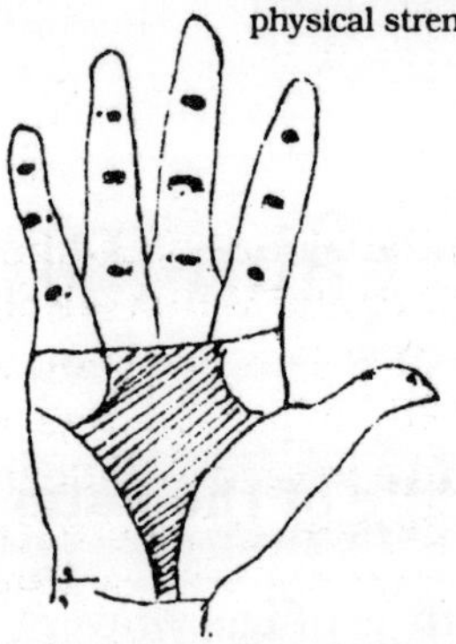

Plain of Mars shows physical strength

Fig. 13-C

According to the treatise on Hindu palmistry, *Samudrika Shastra,* these are called the *Shatrusthan* (the place of the enemy). Some experts in *Samudrika Shastra* call the upper part of the plain as the *Ketusthan* and adjacent to the wrist is the *Rahusthan.*

A few palmists call the lower area of the Plain of Mars as the Plain of Neptune, but most of them do not believe in dividing the plain into two parts. They call the whole of the middle part of the palm as the Plain of Mars. We have designated it as such because of its peculiar features.

Coming to the Plain of Mars, if your client spreads the palm out loosely and finds the middle of it rather full, it indicates that he is full of physical energy. We have mentioned this earlier while speaking of the heavy palm.

If the area is depressed, it indicates lack of physical energy. The palmists of yore thought that a depressed Plain of Mars was indicative of lack of success. Some thought that it represented niggardliness but the modern palmists believe it to represent lack of physical vigour and irritability in nature. There is some truth in both these arguments.

If in addition to the palm being full, the Aggressive and the Defensive Mars are also prominent, then Mars is said to be the predominant planet for that person. Complete predominance of Mars means overdevelopment of all the three areas of Mars. If one or two of the areas are predominant, the person is called partially Martian. Such a Mars should be taken to be normally developed.

Persons with a predominant Mars do not make friends, but confine themselves to a smaller circle of close acquaintances. If the Mounts of Venus, Sun and Mercury are well developed, the circle of friends might be wider.

Let us now come to the special features of both the Aggressive and Defensive Mars.

Aggressive Mars

The Aggressive Mars lies between the Mount of Jupiter and Mount of Venus *(see Fig. 13-B)*. Jupiter and Venus are slightly hot. The area that lies between them is extremely hot, which means that if that area is raised, a person has a hot disposition. Courage and bravery in a person is indicated by the Aggressive Mars. Such a person is interested in adventure. His disposition is the exact opposite of a Saturn character. He cannot hide his feelings — be it of happiness or sorrow. He gives full expression to his feelings. He is an open-hearted person and opts for a career in the army, police, adventure sports like hunting and also competitive sports and games. If the other signs in the palm are favourable, that is, if Jupiter and Sun are favourable, with a fine-textured skin on the palm and a long thumb, the person is likely to become famous and reach a position of power. If the other signs are unfavourable, that is, if the thumb is short, the skin rough and hard, the Head Line defective, the person is quarrelsome and liable to pickup a fight with everyone.

If a person with a prominent Aggressive Mars also has a favourable Mount of Mercury, he engages in business by defeating his business rivals. He dominates his family members.

If the Mount of Moon is well developed, the person is likely to have artistic talent, but the planet Mars influences his artistic creations. Such an artist is more likely to paint pictures of battles than of anything to do with peace.

Saturn, if prominent, alongwith an Aggressive Mars, tends to reduce its virulence and makes a man into a planner. Such a person is adept at planning battle and defence strategies. A prominent Venus increases the sexual urge. A heavy palm tends to increase the typical qualities of an Aggressive Mars,

If the colour of the palm is red, it accentuates the qualities of aggression. A pinkish palm tends to reduce the virulence of such aggression. A person with a prominent Mars does not have a whitish palm.

If a person with a prominent Mars has short nails, he is likely to be more aggressive. Long nails reduce that aggression. A good Head Line and a long thumb are favourable for a man with a prominent Mars. Without them, the aggressive influence of Mars makes a person harmful to society.

Persons with a prominent Aggressive Mars like to stand on their own feet and hate to be dependent on others. They build their own life.

Persons with an overdeveloped Aggressive Mars are dare-devils and are given to quarrelling with others on the slightest pretext. Those with an underdeveloped Aggressive Mars try to avoid quarrels and are apt to surrender easily.

If there is a star or cross on the Aggressive Mars, the person is likely to lose all sense of proportion when angry. If there is a triangle, such persons join the army, the police and are found to excel in competitive sports and games. A grill indicates excess of blood in the brain. A square helps a man to avoid fits of anger.

A person with a prominent Aggressive Mars is liable to fall prey to diseases like improper circulation of blood, breathing, throat and the lungs. He must, therefore, take care and avoid excitement.

Defensive Mars

The Defensive Mars lies between the Mount of Moon and Mount of Mercury (see Fig. 13-A). The Moon is supposed to be a cool planet whereas Mercury is slightly warm. Under the influence of these mounts, the heat of the Mars is reduced.

When the coolness of Mount of Moon and the power of thought associated with Mount of Mercury combine with courage and bravery so typical of Mars, steadfastness results. A person loses his aggressiveness but when he is under attack, he is able to withstand it with courage. A person whose Defensive Mars is slightly raised does not lose courage in the worst of circumstances. He is apt to face the odds with courage at home, in business and in every other field of activity.

If a person has a developed Aggressive Mars in addition to a well-developed Defensive Mars, his courage and bravery are tinged with a spirit of tolerance and discrimination. Such a person does not admit defeat under any circumstances. But, if the Aggressive Mars is developed while the Defensive Mars is underdeveloped, the person might start a quarrel or a fight, but when his opponent hits back, he loses his courage and surrenders. The threats made by a person with developed Aggressive Mars are empty threats.

If the Defensive Mars is strong, the person does not run away from responsibility or a fight, be it at home, his business or any other field. Converse is true in the case of those whose Defensive Mars is underdeveloped. They are the ones who lose hope and courage easily.

Mounts Near the Wrist

Mount of the Moon or Luna

This mount is situated on the palm just above the wrist. It lies below the Defensive Mars. The ancient Hindu palmistry treatise, *Samudrika Shastra* calls this as *Dharmasthana* (the place of righteousness). Western palmistry divides it into three parts. The upper area, just below the Defensive Mars, is called the Upper Moon. The area near the wrist is the Lower

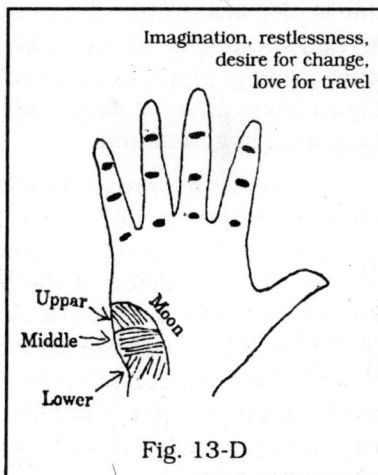

Imagination, restlessness, desire for change, love for travel

Uppar
Middle
Lower
Moon

Fig. 13-D

Moon and the area in between is the Middle Moon. The author's research tells him that its effect is cold *(see Fig. 13-D)*.

Palmists of yore thought that the Moon was connected with water but the new breed of palmists are of the view that if this area is prominent, it indicates a desire for change. A person with a prominent Moon has a sharp imagination but a restless disposition.

No finger represents the Moon and the mount is supposed to be developed if it is raised above the rest of the palm. If it is not raised, but is levelled, it is underdeveloped and if it is very prominent and just out, it is overdeveloped because in that case the thickness of the percussion gives it a rounded appearance *(see Fig. 13-E)*.

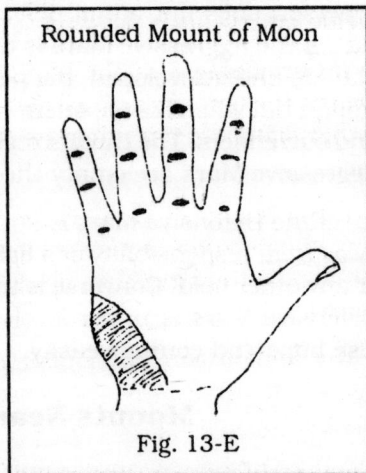

Rounded Mount of Moon

Fig. 13-E

Those with a prominent Moon see with their mind's eyes. If the other signs on the palm are good and the Head Line is also favourable, the person becomes a creative artist. He has the ability to look into the minds of others. If the other signs are bad, the person with a prominent Moon is a daydreamer. There is danger of his being troubled by mental disorders, like insanity.

Persons with a prominent Moon are cool-headed, having less of enthusiasm and zeal. If Sun, Venus, Jupiter and the Aggressive Mars are prominent, they become good mixers and are warm-hearted. If the Mount of Saturn is also well developed, such a person's desire for solitude is high. If Defensive Mars and Mercury are favourable, the person becomes selfish. If Aggressive Mars is positive, the person becomes more active. In short, if the hot and cold mounts are equally prominent, the effect is good and the person is pragmatic.

If the palm of a person with a prominent Mars is hard and substantial, he is able to make progress. If the palm is soft and flabby, he is more active mentally.

Change is the hallmark of the Mount of Moon. That is why persons with a prominent Moon love to travel. If the palm is thick and the Mount of Mercury is well developed, the desire for travel is fulfilled. A person with a flabby hand thinks about journeying abroad, but never gets around to doing it. If Saturn is positive, there is a tendency towards suicide among such persons.

If development of the Mount of Moon is outwards, i.e. towards the percussion (see Fig. 13-E), the person is creative. If other signs are bad, then he is mentally disturbed all the time.

If the Mount of Moon is inclined towards the Defensive Mars, the person uses his imagination for inventing things. If it bends towards the wrist, the person is inclined to daydream.

If a person with a prominent Mount of Moon has long fingers, the standard of his work is high. Small fingers increase the speed of his work.

If the Mount of Moon is underdeveloped, the person can see only those things which are visible to the eye. He has no imagination and cannot enjoy the fine arts.

If there is a cross over the Mount of Moon, the person is liable to die in water according to the older generation of palmists. But according to the new breed, such a situation results in accentuating the person's imagination to such an extent that he might even lose his sanity.

In the older days it was thought that a square on the Mount of Moon signified defence against death in water. Now it is said that such a square is a defence against insanity. If there is a triangle on this mount, the person has a grasp of the occult. A grill signifies discontent, insomnia, restlessness and nervous disorder. About the effect of vertical and horizontal lines on this Mount, we shall speak when we come to the Travel Lines.

Western palmistry divides the Mount of Moon into three parts (see Fig. 13-D). If there are too many transverse or oblique lines on the upper Moon, near the Defensive Mars, the person is liable to face disorders of the throat, chest and the upper parts of the body. If the middle portion is defective, diseases of the stomach and intestines are indicated. In case there are defective signs near the wrist, the danger of diseases of the uterus, scrotum and the kidneys is indicated.

Mount of Venus

The Mount of Venus is situated at the base of the thumb, near the wrist *(see Fig. 13-F)*. According to *Samudrika Shastra*, it is the *Bhratristhan* (the place of the brothers). The author's research leads him to believe that its effect is warm. The Mount of Venus indicates the degree of sexuality, sympathy, love, warm-heartedness, vitality and generosity a person has. If this mount is firm and is spread over an area larger than normal, the person is said to have a prominent Mount of Venus.

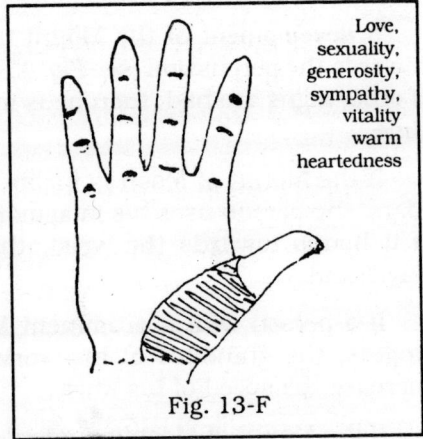

Love, sexuality, generosity, sympathy, vitality warm heartedness

Fig. 13-F

Fingers reveal the characteristics of the mounts which lie at their bases, but the thumb at the base of which the Mount of Venus lies does not represent the qualities of that mount. On the other hand, it represents that part of the brain which is concerned with the sense of discrimination. We have dealt with the effects a long or a short thumb in the chapter on the thumb.

A normal development of the Mount of Venus makes a person healthy and an optimist. Such a person loves his relationship. He worships beauty and has sex appeal. He makes friends easily and has a desire to live a happy life.

An overdeveloped Mount of Venus indicates excessive sexuality and a tendency towards violence. If the Mount of Mercury of such a person is also developed or the little finger is long, or the third phalange of this finger is long or thick,

All the Secrets of Palmistry

he or she would not bother about what is right and what is wrong when satisfying his/her sexual desires.

If an overdeveloped Mount of Venus is accompanied by a developed Aggressive Mars, sexuality is mixed with violence. A good Head Line and a long thumb might prevent such a person from taking to immoral ways, but a short thumb, with a big first phalange and an unfavourable Head Line, show a tendency towards taking to bad traits of the Mount of Venus. We shall deal with the Head Line when we come to that subject.

A person with an underdeveloped Mount of Venus suffers from a sense of insecurity and lacks sympathy for his fellow beings. He has limited physical strength. If there are lines on the Mount of Venus which are parallel to the Life Line, the person does not lack collaborators. We will go into the details of this matter when we come to the lines of the palm.

If there is a grill on the underdeveloped Mount of Venus, the person's sexuality is high, but he does not have the corresponding physical strength to satisfy his sexual desires. Vertical and horizontal lines on the Mount of Venus have other effects too and the reader is advised to persue the chapter on palm lines before he reads a palm.

A flabby Mount of Venus indicates lack of strength. Such persons go out in search of happiness but fail to find it.

If a person with a prominent Mount of Venus has a heavy palm with the third phalange of the fingers thick, he is likely to have more than normal physical strength.

The Mount of Venus is right opposite the Mount of Moon and if both of them are equally raised, forming a small depression in the palm between them, the cool effect of the Moon tends to reduce the heat of Venus. If neither of them is raised, there will not be any depression between them and it indicates lack of physical strength. It also indicates lack in the power of imagination.

If the skin of the palm of the person with a prominent Mount of Venus is thin and flexible, she/he is likely to have finesse in her/his sexual relations. If the skin is thick and rough, his sexual relationships are clumsy and tinged with selfishness. Such persons have little regard for the happiness of others as they are too concerned with their own pleasures.

If there is a grill on an underdeveloped Mount of Venus, it seeks to reduce lack of sexual powers. A grill on a developed mount tends to make it an overdeveloped one. If there are no vertical or horizontal lines on this mount, it indicates that the person does not have true attachment for anybody. Such a person is devoid of sentiments.

A cross on the Mount of Venus indicates a happy marriage. A star, on the other hand, indicates high sexual power. A triangle indicates that the person will think of what he will gain or lose before he decides to marry. A square indicates that the physical strength through the sexual act will not be lost and his health would be safeguarded.

Persons with a prominent Mount of Venus are generally healthy.

Relations Among the Mounts

If one of the mounts is developed and the others are in an underdeveloped state, a person's development is in one direction only which is inauspicious.

In order to reduce the virulence of one overdeveloped mount, it is necessary that the mount which has a contrary effect is also well developed. For example, Jupiter, Sun and Venus have a temperate effect. The effect of the Aggressive Mars is very hot. The heat in Mercury is a little less. Saturn and Moon are cool planets. In short, the three mounts near the thumb have a hot effect and the three at the side of the little finger are cool in effect. The two mounts between them — Saturn is cool while Sun is temperate (see Fig. 13-G). The figure shows horizontal lines on the cool mounts and vertical lines on the hot mounts. The shaded area in between is the Plain of Mars.

If the vertical half of the hand towards the thumb is firm, a person is likely to be more intense than others. A person with such a hand is physically stronger. If in a hand the mounts towards the little finger are stronger or firmer, a person has a sharp brain. He would lack physical strength,

All the Secrets of Palmistry

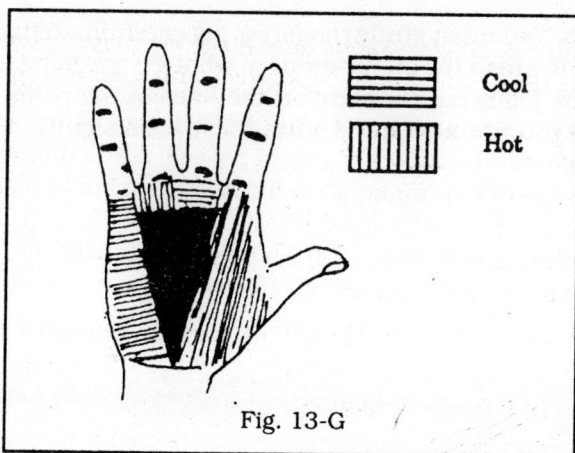
Fig. 13-G

but would have a keen intelligence and a tendency towards selfishness.

The two mounts lying in the middle — Sun and Saturn — are complimentary just as the two near the wrist—Moon and Venus — are.

Complimentary mounts would have to be developed if a person has to have a balanced personality. In other words, if the mounts having a hot effect are developed, some cool mounts have to be equally developed so that the heat could be reduced by their effect. If that does not happen, the development of a person's personality is one-sided, which is not favourable. Cool mounts indicate lack of will power.

If only the mounts representing cool planets are developed, a person cannot give any practical shape to his ideas. If only those representing hot mounts are developed, he cannot think things out. There is thus a likelihood of his falling into a trap of his own making.

We shall come to the chapter regarding remedies which a person can employ to reduce the virulence caused by one-sided development of mounts so that if a client come to you with problems arising out of that, you would be able to advise him what to do in the circumstances.

And with this we conclude the discussion of signs on the

palm. You must study the foregoing carefully so that you are able to grasp the implications of what we are going to discuss in the following chapters on the lines of the palm. It would help you to understand what these lines signify.

Part III

Lines of the Palm or Chiromancy

XIV

Lines of the Palm: A Brief Introduction

Introduction

We have so far dealt with the signs on the palm, the study of which is called chirognomy. We are now about to enter the field of chiromancy, or the lines of the hand.

The lines on the palm are divided into three categories:

1. Main lines

2. Secondary lines

3. Lines of Influence or Chance Lines

In this chapter we shall discuss the main areas where each of these lines lies, leaving the details about them for the following chapters.

The Main Lines

The main lines are three in number (*see Fig. 14-A*).

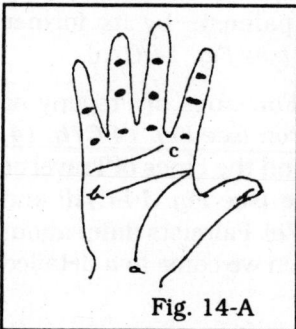

Fig. 14-A

(a) The Life Line indicates the capacity of the muscular body of a person (*see Fig. 14-Aa*).

(b) The Head Line gives an indication about the level of a person's brain (*see Fig. 14-Ab*).

(c) The Heart Line tells about the emotional side of a person (*see Fig. 14-Ac*).

These are called the main lines because they are found in almost every hand. Rare is a hand where one or the other line is missing.

Secondary Lines

These lines are not found in all the hands, but the answers to questions which clients are concerned which are hidden in them. These are:

• The Line of Saturn. It is generally called the Line of Fate or Wealth (see Fig. 14-B/a).

• The Line of Sun or Apollo is secondary to the Line of Saturn. Some palmists call it the Line of Success or Learning (see Fig. 14-B/b).

• The Line of Mercury is also called the Heptica or the Line of Health (see Fig. 14-B/c).

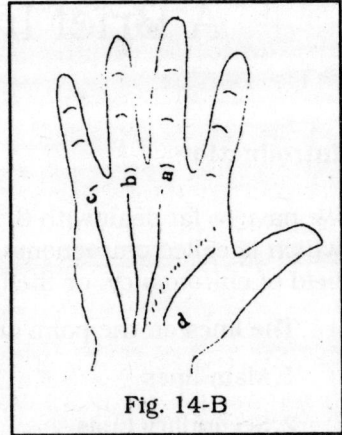

Fig. 14-B

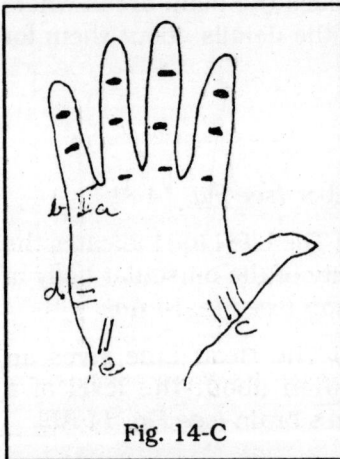

Fig. 14-C

• The Line of Mars is a supporting line to the Life Line. Some palmists believe it is the Line of Influence (see Fig. 14-B/d).

• The Line of Marriage or Line of Association is called by most palmists by its former name (see Fig. 14-C/a).

• For Lines of Progeny or Children (see Fig. 14-C/b, 14-C/c) and the Lines of Travel or Voyage (see Fig. 14-C/d) and (14-C/e). Palmists differ about these lines. We will discuss that when we come to a detailed description of these lines.

All the Secrets of Palmistry

The names of subsidiary lines of the second category are:

• The Girdle of Venus *(see Fig. 14-D/a).*

• The Ring of Saturn *(see Fig. 14-D/b).*

• The Ring of Solomon *(see Fig. 14-D/c).*

• The Intuition Line *(see Fig. 14-D/d).*

• Via lasciva *(see Fig. 14-D/e).* has palmists differ about it. We shall go into the details when we come to this line further on in this text.

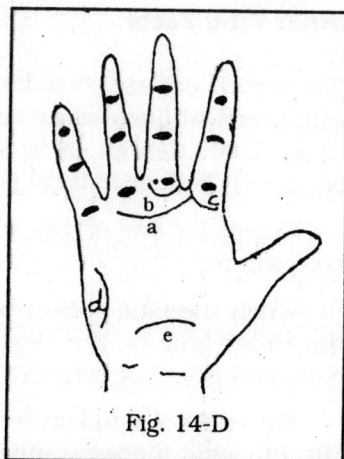

Fig. 14-D

Bracelets or Rascettes

Lines which appear over the palm like a bracelet are called Bracelets and are three or four in number. The first line near the palm is called a Rascette. The other lines behind it is called Bracelets *(see Fig. 14-E).*

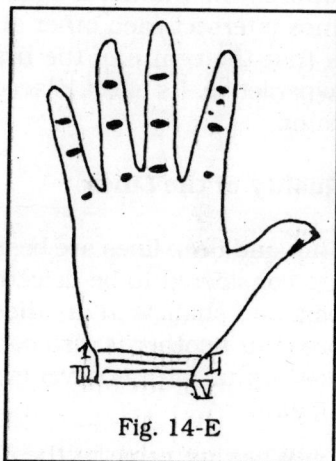

Fig. 14-E

Influence/Chance Lines

Under this category are the lines which have not yet been classified under any nomenclature. They can originate from any mount or any part of the palm or vanish in any other part. These are lines which form grills, triangles, crosses, stars, squares, etc. Their influecne depends on the mount or line near which they are found.

Other Vital Facts

Horizontal lines are considered unfavourable in their effects while vertical lines as favourable. The Head Line and the Heart Line, though horizontal, have no negative effect, because it is their natural position.

Except for one or two places, a cross has a bad effect everywhere.

When the Line of Sun or the Line of Saturn intersects the Heart Line or the Head Line, a cross is formed, but palmistry does not consider it as a cross.

The effect of a grill on the Mount of Venus has a different effect to what it does at other places. The reason is that the vertical lines forming a grill are inclined towards the fingers, which is not a bad sign and if the horizontal lines incline towards the thumb, it again is a positive sign. When these lines intersect each other at the Mount of Venus, the effect is that the centre of the brain connected to this mount is hyperactive. Its effect is according to the other signs on the palm.

Quality of the Lines

Thin and deep lines are best, while broad and shallow lines are considered to be defective. A line which is deep in one part and shallow in another part, or thin at one place and broad at another is also considered to be bad, because the flow of vital force is never even when there are such lines on a palm.

When we come to the details of various lines, we shall deal with the negative and positive aspects of each. Only a general description is sought to be given here.

To find out whether a line is shallow or deep, spread the palm as wide as you can. If a line vanishes in that state or becomes dim, it is considered a shallow line and the one which becomes more prominent is a deep line.

This rule applies to the main and the secondary lines.

All the Secrets of Palmistry

The Lines of Influence are always shallow. If the Lines of Influence are deeper than the main and secondary lines, then they are considered bad.

About the colour of the lines we had mentioned here while talking of the colour of the palm. Pink lines are the best, while black, yellow, deep and red lines are defective. While deciding about the colour, take the colour of the back of the hand into consideration. If the colour of the back of the hand is wheatish, a light pinkish colour of the lines will pass muster. If the colour of the back of the hand is dark, the colour of the lines should be deep pink.

Signs on the Lines

Some signs are found on the lines about which we have spoken in Chapter XI. They are the cross, square, tassel, trident, etc. Some other signs are associated with the lines. Let us understand these before we go into the details of the lines.

A cross formed at the intersection of any line by a Line of Influence comes in the way of the effect of that line. If the line extends beyond the cross, that obstacle is removed. If after a cross, a line becomes dim or stops, the obstacle becomes more serious.

If there is an island on a line, it tends to destroy its effect (*Fig. 14F*). If there is a square with a negative sign it destroys the negative features.

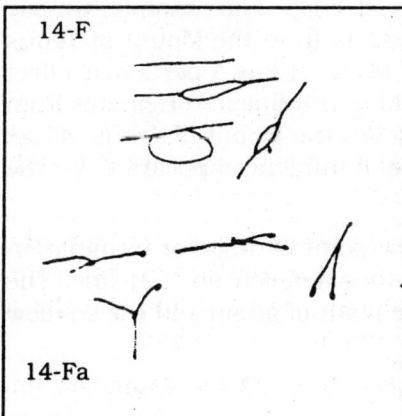

14-F

14-Fa

A forked line (*see Fig. 14-F/a*) indicates the strength of the influence associated with that line. Of the two, whichever part of the fork is deeper has an effect similar to the main line. The shallow part of the fork should be treated like a Line of Influence. The mount towards which a line is inclined has effect on that line.

We have already spoken of the effect of a trident. The branches of the trident going upwards or towards the fingers have a good effect.

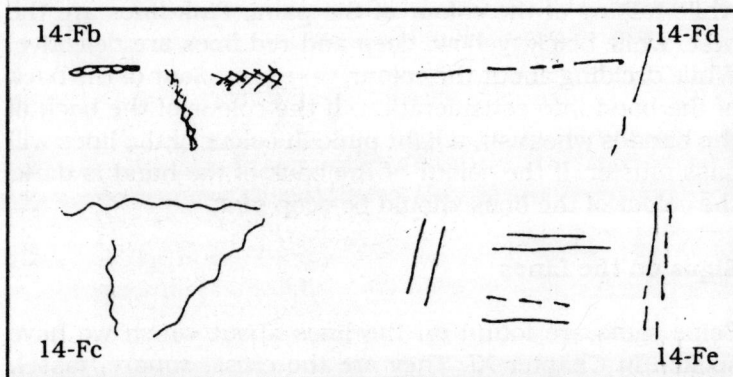

Lines appearing as chains (see Fig. 14-F/b), wavy lines (see Fig. 14-F/c) and broken lines (see Fig. 14-F/d) are defective. If there is a subsidiary line or a parallel line with a defective line (see Fig. 14-F/e) then the defect is removed.

If there is a spot on a line, it indicates a disease connected with that line.

How to Determine the Origin and End of Line of Influence

The place of origin and termination of a main and a secondary line is well-defined, but it is difficult to know where a Line of Influence begins and where it ends. For example, we say that if a Line of Influence starts from the Mount of Venus and reaches the Mounts of Moon, it has a particular effect while at another place, if a Line of Influence originates from the Mount of Moon and reaches the Mount of Venus, it has another effect. But the Line of Influence appears to be the same in these two cases.

When in doubt about the point of origin or termination of a Line of Influence, create a tension on that line. The deeper end of the line is the point of origin and the shallow end is where it terminates.

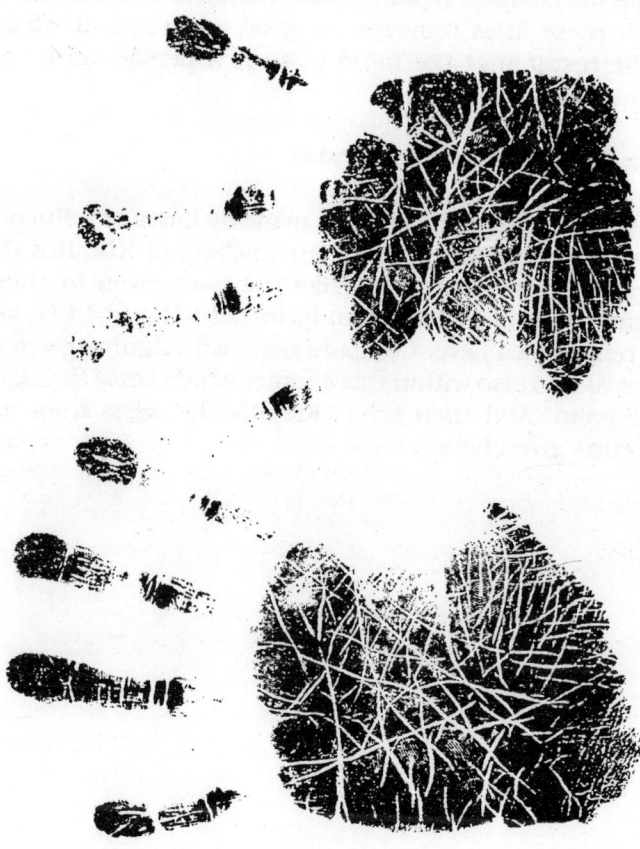

Fig. 14-H

Fig. 14-G

Other Facts about Lines of Influence

If you find many Lines of Influence intersecting each other on a palm, they indicate a multifaceted mind *(see Fig. handprint 14-G and 14-H)*. These are lines which provide material for crosses, squares and triangles. The combined effect of these lines removes the good and the bad effects with the result that the mind of such a person works on many wavelengths.

How to Identify Signs on a Palm

We have given diagrams of signs made by Lines of Influence in Chapter XI and the present one in Chapter XIV. But the signs on a palm are seldom like the ones given in these diagrams. That is why two handprints, 14-G and 14-H, are being reproduced here. Compare them with figures given in chapter XI and also within this chapter which show the signs on the palm. And then try to identify the signs from the handprints given here.

All the Secrets of Palmistry

XV

Lines as Indicators of Life Expectancy and Important Events

Before we go into the details of the lines on the palm, it would be better to learn, how to find the life expectancy and the time of important events in a person's life.

Most palmists agree that the lines can indicate only those events which have a bearing on life. This can be for good or for evil.

They also believe that no definite time or date can be indicated in this regard; only an approximate age can be stated. For example, it could be said that a particular event occurred between the age of 30 to 32 or would take place between these years.

The Line of Saturn indicates a person's wealth and other worldly possessions, his chances of success in trade or employment or the course his career will take. This line starts from (near the wrist) the lower end of the palm. Events which have occurred during childhood would be indicated from the line near the wrist, those of middle age from the middle of the line and the occurrences during old age from the portion of the line which lies near the base of the middle finger *(see Fig. 15-A)*.

The Life Line indicates the physical-capacity of a person's body and family circumstances. It originates between the Mount of Jupiter and the Aggressive Mars and terminates near the wrist. The origin of this line conveys all that has happened during a person's childhood, the middle portion

General rule for calculating age from the Line of Saturn

Old age

Middle age

youth

Childhood

Fig. 15-A

tells about the happenings during youth; and the events of old age are learnt from the end part of the line *(see Fig. 15-B)*.

About finding out the events in a person's life from the Head Line, the Heart Line, the Line of Sun and the Line of Mercury, palmists are not unanimous but the author recomends Cheiro's 'system of seven' following his forty years of experience.

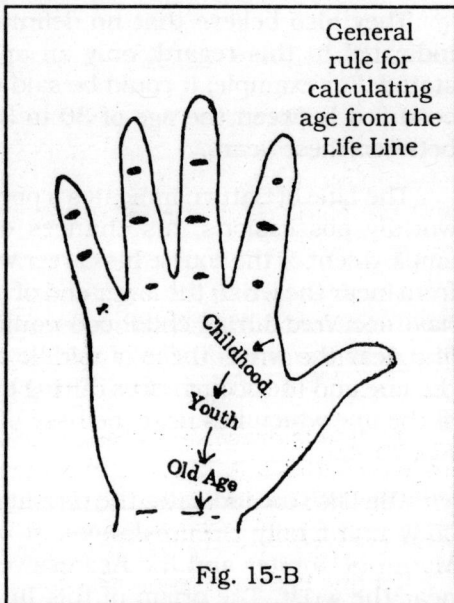

General rule for calculating age from the Life Line

Childhood

Youth

Old Age

Fig. 15-B

Cheiro's System of Seven

Cheiro divides both the Life Line and the Line of Saturn into segments, each representing a span of seven years. *Figures 15-C* (Life Line) and *15-D* (the Line of Saturn) will help you to understand this rule.

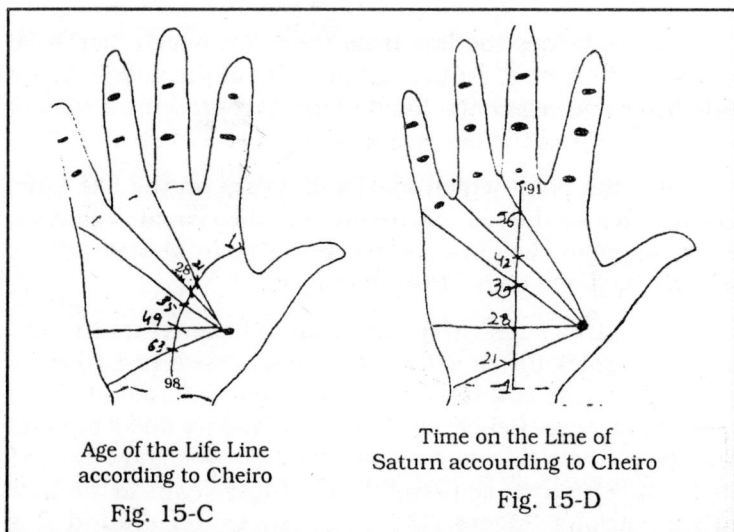

Age of the Life Line according to Cheiro

Fig. 15-C

Time on the Line of Saturn accourding to Cheiro

Fig. 15-D

A line is drawn at the centre of the Mount of Venus going up to the first bracelet of the wrist. The point at which this line intersects the Life Line represents an age of 63 years and the point where it intersects the Line of Saturn is the age of 21 years.

A horizantal straight line is drawn from the centre of the Mount of Venus to the percussion of the palm. The junction of this line with the Life Line gives the age of 49 years. Its intersection at the Line of Saturn shows the age of 28 years.

If a line is drawn from the centre of the Mount of Venus up to the outer edge of the base of the little finger, its junction with the Life Line and the Line of Saturn indicates an age of 35 years on both these lines.

If a line is drawn from the centre of the Mount of Venus to the base of the little finger and to the middle of the base of the ring finger, the Life Line indicates an age of 28 years and the Line of Saturn an age of 42 years.

The line drawn from the centre of the Mount of Venus till the middle of the middle finger and the ring finger shows an age of 21 years on the Life Line and 56 years on the Line of Saturn.

Cheiro divides the line from the point which marks 56 years on the Line of Saturn till the base of the middle finger into five equal segments. Each segment represents a span of seven years and the last segment ends at 91 years.

After the point which marks 63 years on the Life Line, Cheiro divides the rest of the line into five equal segments. Each segment, he says, represents a span of seven years and the last one ends at 98 years.

The author's research leads him to believe that in sofar as the Line of Saturn and the Life Line are concerned, Cheiro's seven-year rule is the most accurate one but, as has been the author's experience, students of palmistry find if difficult to follow Cheiro's rule because they do not know how to draw lines from the centre of the Mount of Venus to the base of the various fingers. The best way to get around this difficulty is to accept that the middle of the Line of Saturn represents an age of 35 years (see Fig. 15-E) and also to suppose that the age near the wrist, as shown by the Line of Saturn, is one year (even though that line may not begin from there) and that at the end of the line near the base of the middle finger, it is 91 years (never mind if the line does not extend to that part of the palm). If more space is allotted to two spans of seven years each between 21 and 35 years and less to the seven- year span for the rest of the Line of Saturn, it would suffice.

Similarly, from the middle of the Life Line where the age is supposed to be 35 years (see Fig. 15-E) till the end of the palm near the wrist, where the Life Line usually ends, put a mark showing 98 years (even if the line does not extend till that point). The age at the beginning of the line should be taken to be one year. But both these methods are mere expedients; we have mentioned them to ease the pressure on the minds of the students so that they can grasp this

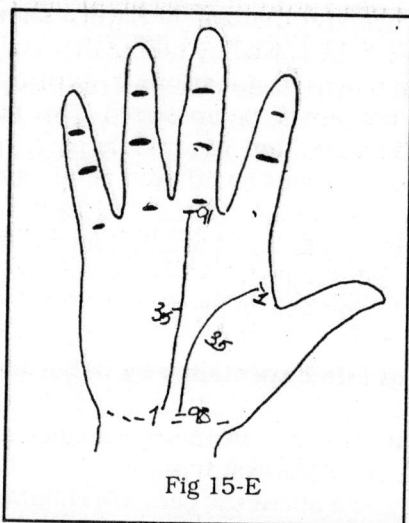

Fig 15-E

rule easily. They should, again and again, try to use the rule according to which the Mount of Venus is taken as the centre from where the line is drawn. Calculation of age would be more accurate if that is done.

In short, according to this rule, the important phase of life as evidenced by the Line of Saturn is 21 to 56 and on the Life Line it is between 21 and 63 years of age. That is why more space is given to this part of life and rightly too. Students must, therefore, follow Cheiro's rule to calculate the life span of an individual.

Another Difficulty

Many times you will find that the beginning of the Line of Saturn and the Life Line is one (see Fig. 15-F) and the student is unable to understand whether he should mark that end according to the Life Line or the Line of Saturn, because the point at which these two lines meet, the Life Line

Fig. 15-F

indicates old age and the Line of Saturn shows childhood. This problem can be solved by taking that single line as the Line of Saturn where questions regarding wealth and employment, etc. are to be answered. This part of the line represents childhood and the middle part, youth. If there are any questions about health and family matters, there a single line (where the Life Line and that of Saturn become one) should be treated as the Life Line. In that case, the middle of the palm represents youth and the end of the line near the wrist signifies old age.

Indications of Life Expectancy by Other Lines

In so far as the Heart and the Head Lines are concerned, most palmists are of the view that the Mount of Jupiter should be studied to learn about the person's childhood; the Mount of Saturn for youth; the Mount of Apollo for middle age; and the Mount of Mercury for old age. The author's view is that if the Heart Line is short, it indicates lack of sentimentality and the shortness of the Head Line signifies lack of mental capacity in a person.

Some Clarifications

If the Life Line is short, some palmists believe that the person would die in his youth or middle age. But this is not the case. One must consult other lines too before one makes a prediction. If the other main lines are positive, one should take it that even if the Life Line is not present or is indistinct, it signifies that the person would be physically weak or will face family problems. He may continue to live because of the strength of his head and heart. Even if the Head Line and the Heart Line are short, one should not hasten to conclude that the person would die soon. If you read the text of this work carefully, you would get the answers to most of the questions that bother you.

If the Line of Saturn is not seen in a palm, do not, for God's sake, think that the man is unlucky. There are many other signs which signify luck. We will come to these things at their appropriate place.

We have only given a rough outline of the lines of the

All the Secrets of Palmistry

palm in Chapter XIV so that the readers know the names of the lines and their location. The rule for calculating the life span would be needed by the student every time he reads a palm and that is why we have dilated upon it here. The student must keep in mind the details given so far and only then he should go into the finer details regarding the lines of the palm.

XVI

Three Main Lines

The three main pillars of human life are: the muscular body; the nervous system or the brain; and the heart as the seat of sentiments.

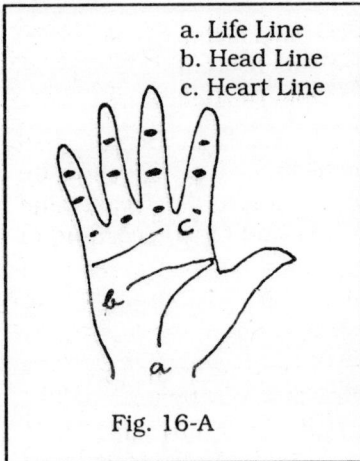

a. Life Line
b. Head Line
c. Heart Line

Fig. 16-A

The level of activity of the three systems is reflected in the three main lines of the palm (see Fig. 16-A).

The health or the physical body can be read from the Life Line. The Head Line tells about the level of activity of the brain in an individual and the Heart Line shows whether a person is sentimental or devoid of finer feelings.

Practitioners of the ancient Indian science of palmistry, as given in *Samudrika Shastra,* call these lines with different names—the Life Line according to them is the *Gotra Rekha,* or, according to some, it is the *Pitri Rekha;* the Head Line is called the *Dhana Rekha* or *Matri Rekha* and the Heart Line is called the *Ayu Rekha.*

Cheiro gives the pride of place to the Head Line, because, he argues, man is superior to all other living beings as he has the brain or intelligence which animals lack.

According to Benham, the most important line is the

Heart Line because it is nearest to the index finger, and is the conduit through which vitality enters the human body. It is that vital force, says Benham, which first of all forms the Heart Line.

Most palmists think that the most important of all lines of the palm is the Life Line, because it is found in most palms, whereas the Heart Line and the Head Line might be missing from some palms.

According to studies undertaken by palmists, the Heart Line is missing from about 2 per cent of the palms studied and the Head Line is found missing from 1 per cent of the palms. But no instance can be found in which both these lines were missing from a palm.

A question arises as to what should be done in case there is only one of these horizontal lines on the palm? Should it be treated as the Head Line or Heart Line (see Fig. 16-B)?

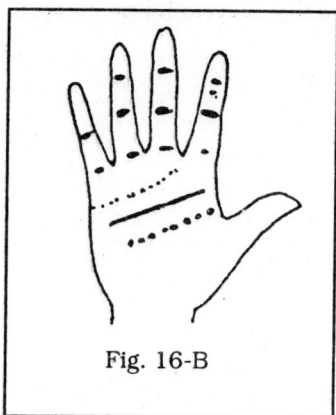

Fig. 16-B

The answer to this question is that the line be named either the Heart Line or the Head Line according to its placement on the palm. If it is near the base of the fingers, it should be treated as the Heart Line. If it lies between the Aggressive Mars and the Defensive Mars, it should be treated as the Head Line. We have spoken of the two Mars when we talked about the map of the hand.

If the path of such a single line lies between the paths of the Head Line and the Heart Line, it should be treated as an amalgam of the two lines. It has the qualities of both these lines.

Western palmists call such a single line as the Simian Line, because it is found in apes who are closest to man by nature. Some of them treat it as the Line of Bestiality, but, the author believes that it can be treated as such only if the palm is hard, the hand is small with small fingers and thumb and a long first phalange on the thumb.

If there is a Heart Line in a palm, but the Head Line is missing, it means that the person is impulsive and such a person acts without thought because he does not have the capacity to think out the consequences of his actions. But, if the Heart Line is missing and the Head Line is positive, it means that sentiments have no place in that man's life and he acts after calculating his profit and loss only.

Before we go into the details of these lines, it should be stated here that these lines are to be found in almost all the palms. If there are only these three lines on a palm, it means that the life of that individual will be without any change for the better or for worse — it would be a long continuum of sameness. In other words, such a person lives his life without any ambition. Secondary lines and Lines of Influence, in addition to these three lines, make the mind active; they also indicate fluctuations, for better or for worse. We will come to such fluctuations when we discuss each line in detail in the following chapters.

XVII

The Life Line

The Life Line is semi-circular in shape; it indicates a person's physical capacity and ability to maintain family relations. It originates from any of the following points:

• The Mount of Jupiter *(see Fig. 17-A)*.

• From a point between the Mount of Jupiter and Aggressive Mars *(see Fig. 17-B)*.

• The Aggressive Mars *(see Fig. 17-C)*.

Fig. 17-A   Fig. 17-B   Fig. 17-C

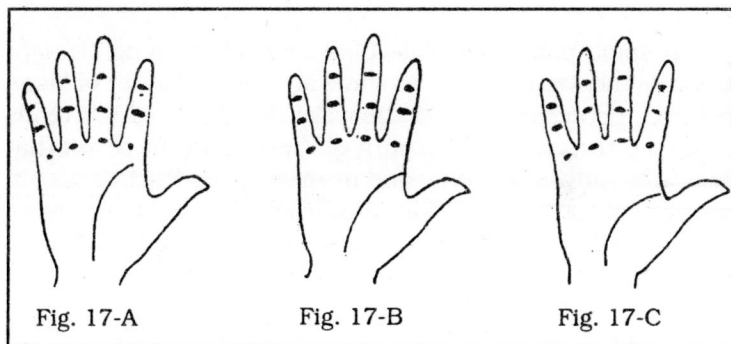

Starting from any of the above three points, the Life Line moves towards the wrist while it encircles the Mount of Venus.

If it originates from the Mount of Jupiter, the person is ambitious and if the other signs are good, he fulfils his ambitions. If a person's Life Line originates from a point between the Mount of Jupiter and the Aggressive Mars, he is likely to be balanced, but if it starts from the Aggressive Mars, he is sure to be aggressive in his behaviour.

In some palms, the line turns towards the base of the Mount of Venus limiting the area of that mount *(see Fig. 17-D)*. In such cases if the Mount of Venus is flat, the person is likely to have less of virility and a weak sexuality. If there is a mesh or a grill on a flat Mount of Venus, sexuality remains, but physical energy is in short supply. A restricted area of the Mount of Venus also indicates less of human sympathy too.

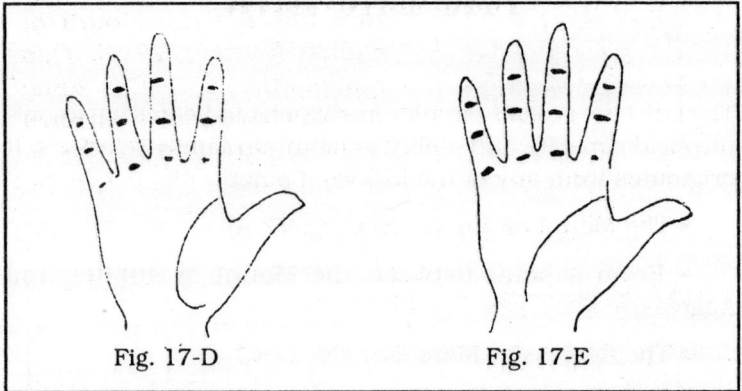

Fig. 17-D   Fig. 17-E

In some palms, the Life Line instead of going straight towards the wrist, envelopes some area of the Mount of Moon before it proceeds towards the wrist *(see Fig. 17-E)*. It tends to extend the area of the Mount of Venus with the result that sexuality, physical energy and human sympathy increase in proportion to the extension of that area. If in such a palm, the Plain of Mars is prominent or the palm is thick and heavy, both sexuality and aggressiveness tend to increase.

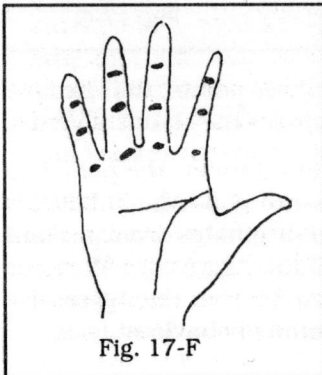

Fig. 17-F

If the Life Line passes through the middle of the palm and goes straight to the wrist, it indicates a balanced personality with good health, sympathy and a balance in human relationships.

In some palms, the beginning of the Life Line merges with the Head Line *(see Fig. 17-F)*. Such a person is

All the Secrets of Palmistry

careful and wide awake and does not undertake anything which has an element of risk involved in it. Where the Life Line merges with the Head Line, the person is dominated by his family in early age.

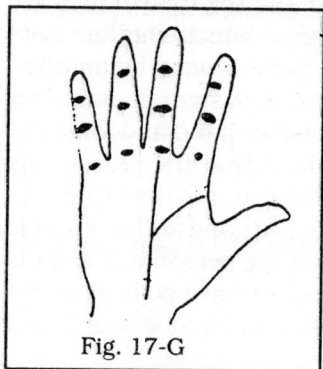

Fig. 17-G

In some palms the Life Line is short, but the Line of Saturn originating from the wrist touches the Life Line and goes towards the Mount of Saturn (see Fig. 17-G). This combination indicates some special change in a person's life. The period when this is likely to take place can be calculated from the Line of Saturn.

If the Life Line is broken but the next part of it begins before the point of break (see Fig. 17-H a, 17-H b), it indicates a special change in life. Sometimes the Life Line is short, but the Line of Mars, parallel to it, is long (see Fig. 17-I). This helps to make up for the short Life Line. It also indicates that the wife/

Fig. 17-H

husband of such a person or his/her parents would help him till the Line of Mars runs parallel to the Life Line. The point of time when this is likely to happen can be calculated with reference to the Life Line.

According to an old belief the length of the Life Line is indicative of the longevity of a person's life but researchers have come to the conclusion

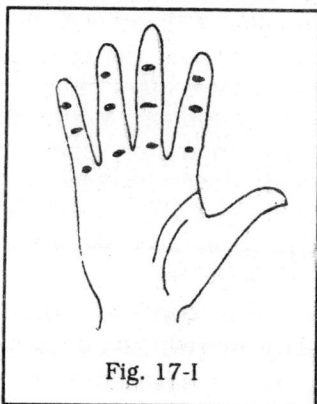

Fig. 17-I

that it can happen only if the Head Line, the Heart Line and the Line of Mercury are helpful. If the Life Line is short in both the right and the left palms and the Head Line and the Heart Line are also short, it indicates a short life. But if only the Life Line is short, but the Head and the Heart Lines are long, it only indicates that the age at which the Life Line ends, the physical energy of the person would diminish. Strength of the heart and the nervous system sustain life, but if the Life Line is short in the passive hand and long and deep in the active one, you can take it that the person has improved his health by his own efforts. If it is the other way round, that is, unfavourable in the active hand and favourable in the passive hand, it indicates that the person has lost his health because of his own mistakes. We have pointed out in an earlier, chapter that the active hand is that with which a person writes.

A defective line means a broken line; one which has a chain or is wavy or has islands on it, or is deep at one place and faint on others or is composed of many pieces. A person might lose his health in his lifetime which is indicated by the above faults in the Life Line.

We would now discuss the effects such faults have on a person's life. If you want to know the name of the disease which will strike a person with a defective Life Line, look at the various mounts. A person with a prominent Mount of Jupiter is likely to suffer from diseases of the digestive system; one with a prominent Aggressive Mars might fall victim to paralysis; one with a prominent Mount of Saturn can apprehend diseases of the bones; a prominent Mount of Apollo or Sun can lead to diseases of the heart and the eyes; a prominent Mount of Mercury and Defensive Mars indicate diseases of the nervous system and a prominent Mount of Venus shows disorders of the sexual organs or venereal diseases. If the upper part of the Mount of Moon is defective, that is, if the lines are broken or there is a grill over it, diseases of the throat and the respiratory organs are possible. If the middle part of the Mount of Moon is defective, then disorders of the intestines are indicated and a defective lower Moon presages disorders of the kidney and the reproductive organs.

The defective Life Line can be read only with reference to the mounts. If there are faults in any particular mount, disorders connected with that are liable to strike the person at a point of time in life indicated by the Life Line.

If the Life Line is broken in the middle, it indicates a crisis or a serious mishap. The lines of the other palm must be read before a correct assessment can be made. If the subsidiary line near the break in the Life Line is helpful, the bad effect of the fault is not of much consequence (see Fig. 17-J). A square also tends to offset the evil effects of the fault. If the line improves after the break, it indicates that the person's health would improve after that period of time, but if improvement after the break is missing, then the health may never improve.

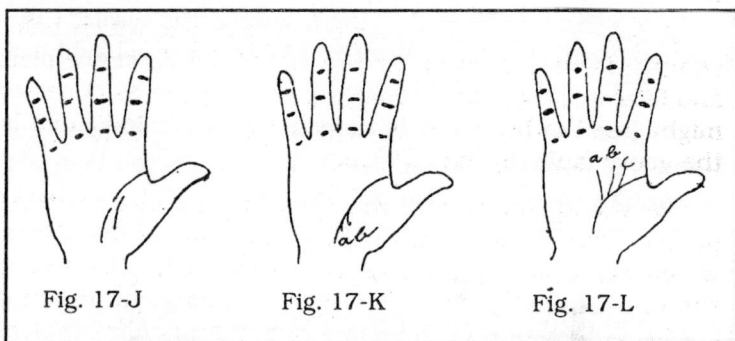

Fig. 17-J   Fig. 17-K   Fig. 17-L

A Life Line branching towards the wrist indicates loss of physical vigour at that age (see Fig. 17-Ka, Kb).

If the line branches out upwards (that is, towards the fingers), it is an indication of success at that point of time in one's life (see Figs. 17-La, 17-Lb, 17-Lc). The mount towards which these branches are inclined has a predominating influence.

Branches of the Life Line going towards the Mount of Moon indicate a desire for change of place (see Fig. 17-Ma, Mb). If along with this, the first phalange of the thumb is long and straight, the palm is firm, then the desire for change of place is fulfilled.

Fig. 17-M

But if the palm is flabby and soft and the second phalange of the thumb is longer than the first, the desire does not get fulfilled.

Fig. 17-N

If the Life Line is full but its end split into two branches *(see Fig. 17-N)*, with one of them going towards the Mount of Luna and the other towards the Mount of Venus, the point to be noted is which of the branches is deep. If the branch going towards the Mount of Luna is deep *(See Fig. Na)*, the person either goes to live abroad or settles there, but if the branch going towards the Mount of Venus is deeper *(see Fig. 17-Nb)*, there is likelihood of his/her coming back home.

A branch of the Life Line which runs parallel to it and enters the Mount of Venus shows that the person is under somebody's thumb *(see Fig. 17-O)*.

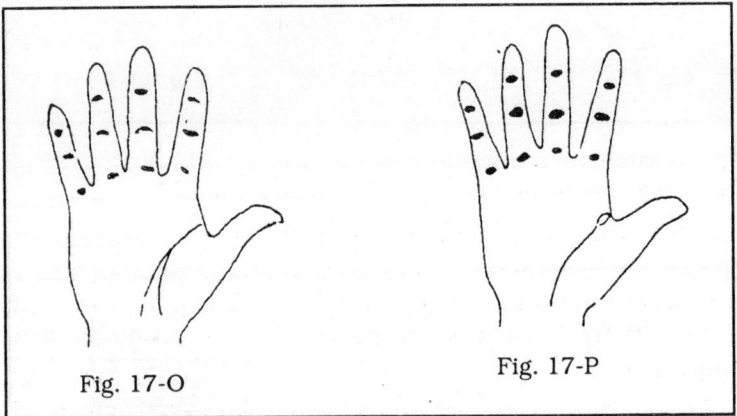

Fig. 17-O

Fig. 17-P

If there is an island at the beginning of the Life Line, there is some mystery surrounding his birth *(see Fig. 17-P)*. If there is an island elsewhere on the Life Line, it indicates that the person would suffer from some disease. The duration of the illness will depend on the length of the island. In order to find out the disease that the person will suffer from, look

All the Secrets of Palmistry

at the mounts on the palm and see which of them is defective. We have seen in the chapter on mounts the various diseases associated with the various mounts.

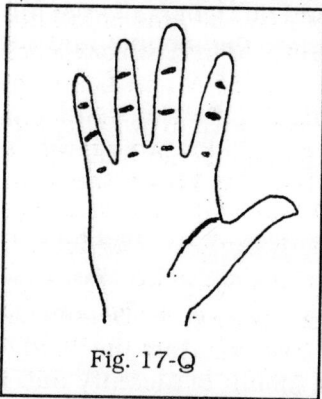
Fig. 17-Q

If the depth of the Life Line gradually diminishes and vanishes before it reaches its full length, it indicates that the physical energy of the person would diminish gradually due to family problems (see Fig. 17-Q).

A double Life Line indicates excellent health.

If oblique lines emanating from the Mount of Venus intersect the Life Line, the person is likely to face problems created by members of the family of the opposite sex (see Fig. 17-Ra). Lines emanating from the Aggressive Mars and intersecting the Life Line indicate problems created by the members of the family of the same sex (see Fig. 17-Rb). These are called worry lines.

If these worry lines in addition to intersecting the Life Line intersect the Line of Saturn too (see Fig. 17-Sa), they tend to harm financially and a person might lose his means of livelihood. If they intersect the Line of Sun too, the person might lose his reputation (see Fig. 17-Sb). If these lines end near the Life Line instead of intersecting it, it indicates anxieties and worries (see Fig. 17-Sc).

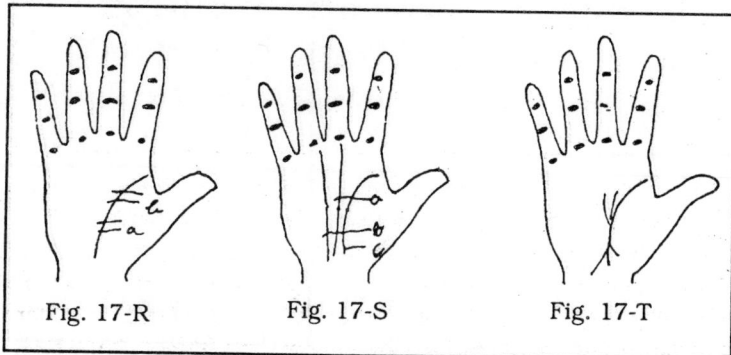

Fig. 17-R   Fig. 17-S   Fig. 17-T

If there is a star on the Life Line, there is a possibility of the person undergoing surgery at that age. A cross or a black spot on the Life Line indicates a possibility of the person meeting with an accident. If the spot is red, the possibility of illness is indicated. In order to find out which disease the person is likely to suffer from, study the mounts and the nails.

If the Life Line branches out both upwards and downwards, it indicates that the person would fulfil all his desires (see Fig. 17-T).

A shallow Life Line indicates illness all through life.

Cheiro believes that the point at which the Line of Mercury touches (see Fig. 17-U) or intersects (see Fig. 17-Ua) the Life Line, it indicates the time of death. He says that the point of origin of the Mercury Line is the Mount of Mercury and it ends at the wrist or the Mount of Venus or the Mount of

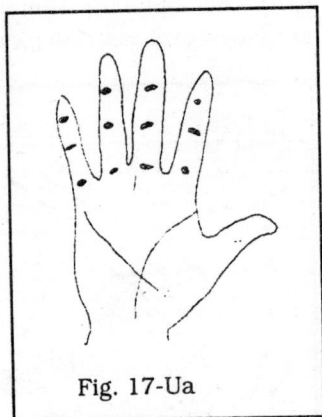

Fig. 17-U

Fig. 17-Ua

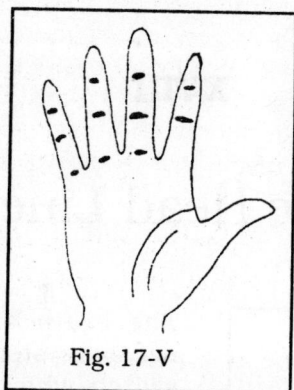
Fig. 17-V

Moon.

But most other palmists disagree with Cheiro in this respect. They believe that the point of origin of the Line of Mercury is the wrist, the Mount of Venus, the Mount of Moon or the end of the Life Line and that it ends at the Mount of Mercury. The author agrees that the Mount of Mercury is a terminal point on the Line of Mercury. According to his finding, the Line of Mercury is not fatal for life. He also says that if the Line of Mercury crosses the Life Line and goes to the Mount of Mercury, it is beneficial for his success. Details are given in Chapter XXII regarding the Line of Mercury.

XVIII

The Head Line

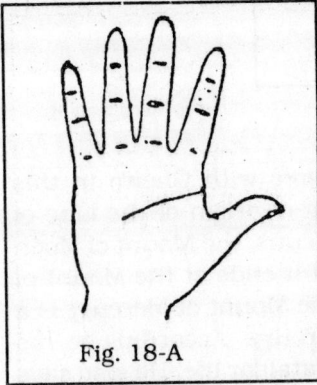

Fig. 18-A

The brain or the central nervous system is like a main switch which controls the actions of the body. Nature has designed a hard skull to protect the brain. Since we cannot open that skull to find out what is going on in there, the best way is to consult the Head Line on the palm and its natural position is shown in *Fig. 18-A*.

If the Head Line is good, it could counter the bad effects of other lines but if it is defective, there is a strong possibility of the defects of the other lines increasing.

In view of the importance of the Head Line, the famous palmist Cheiro has given it the pride of place in his scheme of things. He thinks that it is the most important among the main lines of the palm. Other palmists read the Line of Saturn to find out the financial status of a person and the Line of Sun to see whether he would achieve success in life. The author's advice is to study the Head Line before reaching a final conclusion.

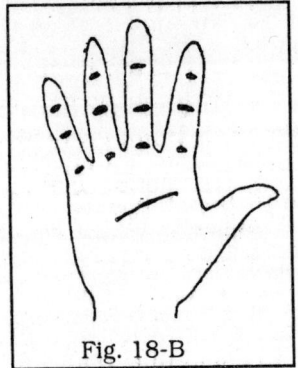

Fig. 18-B

A short Head Line *(see Fig. 18-B)* indicates diminished cerebral capacity. A long, deep Head Line indicates an excellent brain.

All the Secrets of Palmistry

A thin, deep and clear Head Line, which is long, indicates a good memory and an excellent mind. A defective Head Line points to some deficiency in the mind. A person with such a line should not exert his mind too much.

The points of origin on the Head Line are:

• The base of the Mount of Jupiter (see Fig. 18-Ca).

• A point between the Mount of Jupiter and the Aggressive Mars (see Fig. 18-Cb).

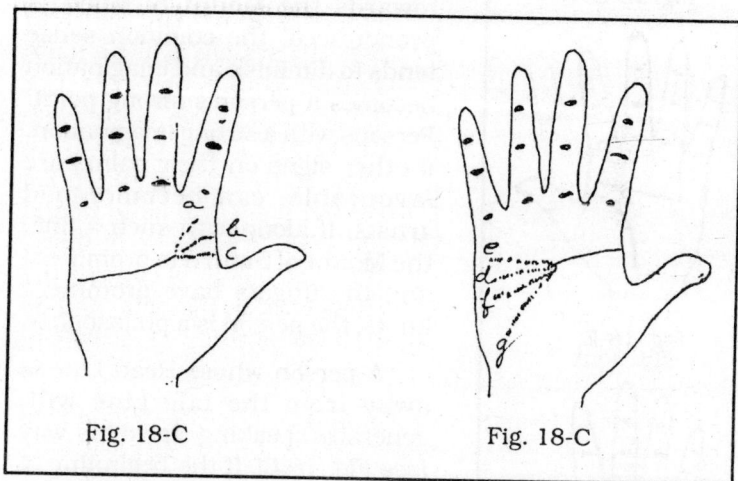

Fig. 18-C   Fig. 18-C

•· The Aggressive Mars (see Fig. 18-Cc).

The points of termination on the Head Line are:

• Defensive Mars (see Fig. 18-Cd).

• Through Defensive Mars to the Mount of Mercury, which is slightly raised (see Fig. 18-Ce).

• Through Defensive Mars and inclined towards the Mount of Moon (see Fig. 18-Cf).

• The Mount of Moon (see Fig. 18-Cg).

A person whose Head Line originates from the Mount of Jupiter has great capacity for work.

If the Head Line slightly touches the Life Line and then separates and goes towards the Defensive Mars, it is

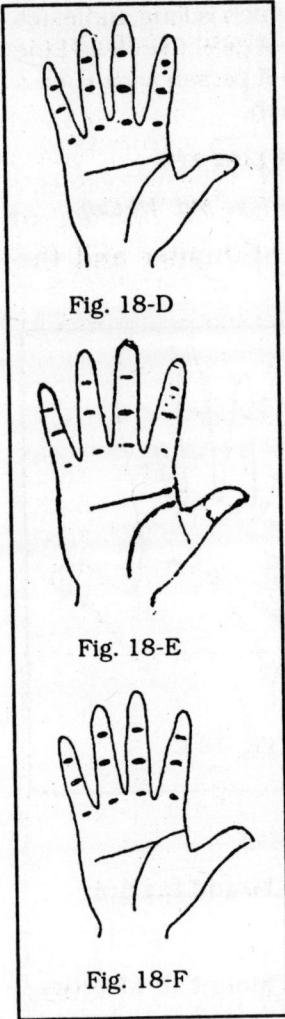

Fig. 18-D

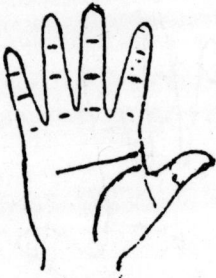

Fig. 18-E

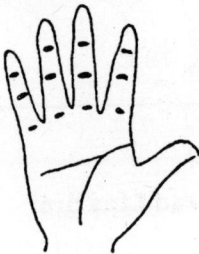

Fig. 18-F

indicative of the presence of common sense (see Fig. 18-D). But such persons usually lack imagination.

If the Head Line inclines slightly towards the Mount of Moon, there is a healthy combination of common sense and imagination. If the inclination towards the Mount of Moon is pronounced, the common sense tends to diminish and imagination becomes a person's strong point. Persons with a strong imagination, if other signs on their palms are favourable, can become good artists. If along with such a line, the Mount of Saturn is prominent and the fingers have prominent knots, the person is a philosopher.

A person whose Head Line is away from the Life Line will, generally speaking, have his way (see Fig. 18-E). If the beginning of the line is more distant from the Life Line, carelessness would grow into recklessness. He would be a spendthrift and insist on having his way in all things. If the thumb of such a person is short, his carelessness tends to increase and, conversely, a long thumb reduces the reckless spirit. A correct assessment can, of course, be made only after the thumb and the mounts have been studied thoroughly.

If the Head Line and the Life Line originate as a single line and after a short distance separate to go in their natural directions, it indicates a person without any self-confidence (see Fig. 18-F) during childhood. They are called 'shrinking violets'. When the Head Line separates from the Life Line,

All the Secrets of Palmistry

self-confidence returns. As to when that will happen can be calculated with reference to the Life Line.

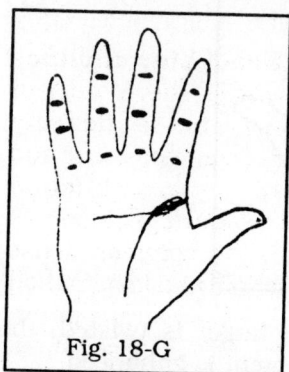
Fig. 18-G

If the Life Line and the Head Line originate like a twisted rope, the person is likely to lose hope easily and become despondent (see Fig. 18-G). But, if in such a palm, the Defensive Mars is developed, this fault tends to diminish.

If the Head Line and the Life Line originate separately but there are short lines between them, the person is liable to be careless and indecisive (see Fig. 18-H).

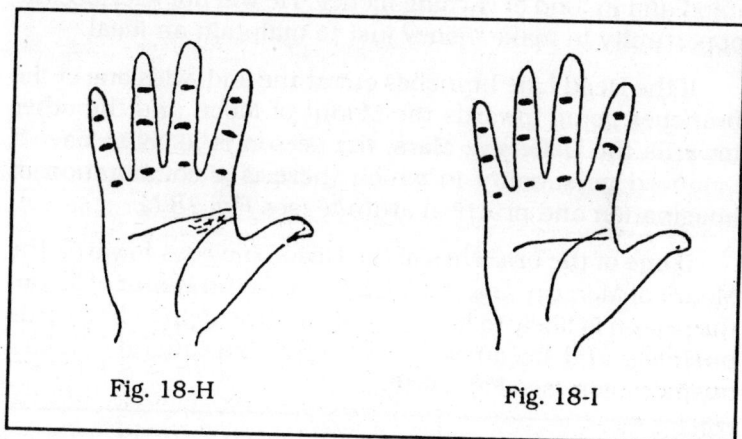
Fig. 18-H   Fig. 18-I

If the Head Line originates from the Aggressive Mars, the person is liable to be violent. Such a person does not mix with others, nor can he make friends (see Fig. 18-I).

If the Head Line inclines towards the Mount of Mercury he uses his talents for trade and for his own betterment (see Fig. 18-J). If the Mount of Mercury is defective or the little finger is long, a person might even commit a crime for

Fig. 18-J

personal advancement. If the little finger is twisted, the tendency towards personal advancement is enhanced.

If the end of the Head Line branches out at the end with one of the branches going towards the Mount of Mercury and the other towards the other side of the palm (see Fig. 18-K), then the person is likely to have a practical bent of mind and in fond of earning money. He will not sacrifice the opportunity to make money just to maintain an ideal.

If the Head Line branches out at the end, with one of the branches going towards the Mount of Moon and the other towards the Defensive Mars, the person is likely to have a balanced personality in which there is a combination of imagination and practical attitude (see Fig. 18-L).

If one of the branches of the Head Line goes towards the Mount of Mercury and the other towards the Mount of Moon, the person is likely to have an imaginative approach towards business and becomes a successful bureaucrat/trader/businessman (see Fig. 18-M).

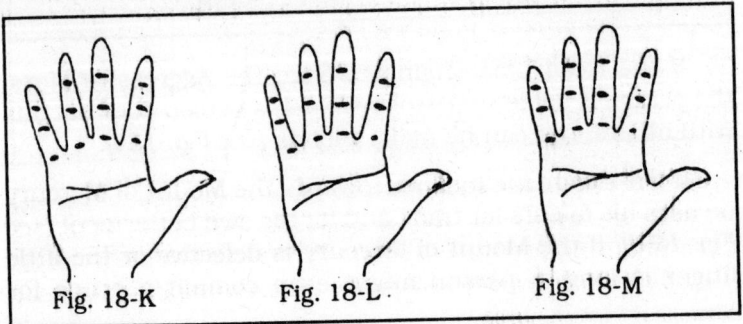

Fig. 18-K   Fig. 18-L   Fig. 18-M

All the Secrets of Palmistry

If the Head Line has three branches, one going towards the Mount of Mercury, the second towards the Defensive Mars and the third towards the Mount of Moon (see Fig. 18-N) the person is likely to have extra mental energy. He has a lot of common sense.

If the beginning of the Head Line is straight, but the last part inclines towards the Mount of Moon, the person is likely to be practical during the early part of his life and acquire a love for fine arts in the evening of his life (see Fig. 18-O). If the fingers are knotty, he is likely to be interested in philosophy.

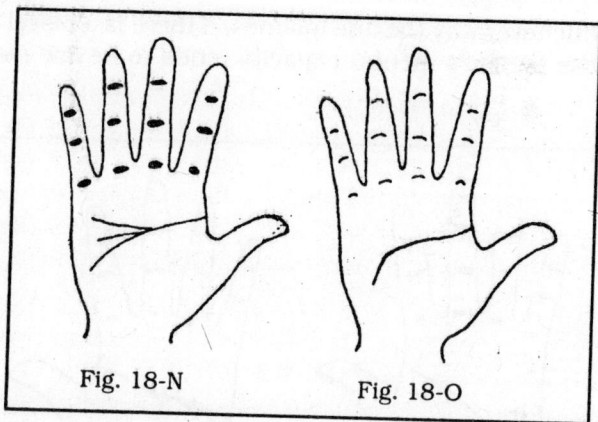

Fig. 18-N   Fig. 18-O

If the Head Line inclines towards the Mount of Luna from the very beginning (see Fig. 18-P), the person has a keen imagination (but be sure to identify the Head Line properly because if it has a sharp incline, it resembles the Life Line). If along with the Head Line inclining towards the Mount of Moon, the other signs of the palm are good, the person is likely to be a literature or an artist. If the other signs are not favourable, he is more of a day-dreamer

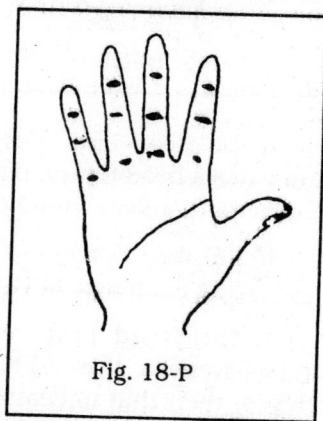

Fig. 18-P

than a man of action. If along with this, the Mount of Saturn is prominent, the person might lose his sanity and commit suicide. An island, a cross or a star on the Mount of Moon increases the defects of the Head Line.

If the Head Line inclining towards the Mount of Moon crosses it and reaches near the wrist, it is a sign of evil things or disasters in life. Such a person might lose his sanity or commit suicide *(see Fig. 18-Q)*.

If the Head Line is shallow at some places and deep at others, the person lacks concentration of mind. If the line is twisted like a rope, it has the same effect.

Whichever way the line inclines, if there is a tassel at the end, the person's mental capacity tends to be low *(see Fig. 18-R)*.

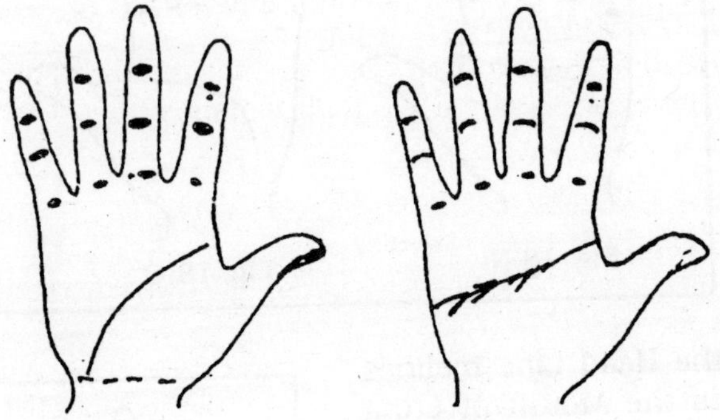

Fig. 18-Q   Fig. 18-R

If the Head Line is fragmented in both the palms, it indicates a head injury. If it is broken only in one palm, then the person suffers from headaches *(see Fig. 18-S)*.

If a broken Head Line is overlapped by another, it is an indication of change of views in a person *(see Fig. 18-T)*.

If the Head Line resembles a chain, it indicates indecisiveness. If in addition to being like a chain, it also slopes, then that indicates a tendency towards depression. A line with an island indicates anxiety and weakness of the nervous system. If it is found in both the palms, the tendency

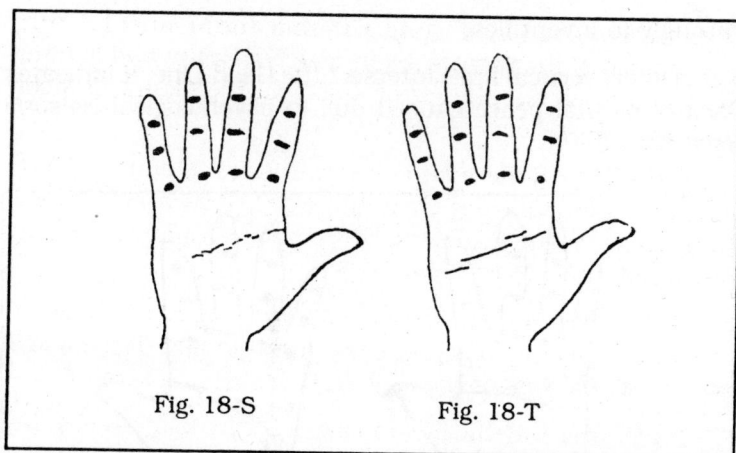

Fig. 18-S   Fig. 18-T

is inherited from the parents. Samples of such chains and islands have been dealt with in an earlier chapter.

A triangle on the line indicates a scientific bent of mind.

A Head Line composed of small lines indicates weakness of the nervous system and a flighty disposition (see Fig. 18-U).

If there is a depression on the Head Line which resembles a point, it indicates a tendency towards worrying. If there is a star at the end of a straight Head Line, it is indicative of a disease of the brain. The nature of the disorder can be found if you study the mounts. A person with prominent Mounts of Saturn, Mercury and Moon is liable to fall prey to paralysis and if the Mounts of Jupiter,

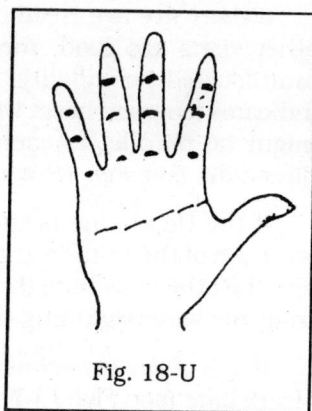

Fig. 18-U

Venus, Apollo and the Aggressive Mars are prominent, they indicate severe headaches because of an excessive amount of blood in the brain.

If there is a star on the Head Line which inclines towards the Mount of Moon, the person is liable to use his imagination wrongly to invent lies.

If short vertical lines intersect the Head Line, it indicates lack of mental peace caused due to psychological reasons (*see Fig. 18-V*).

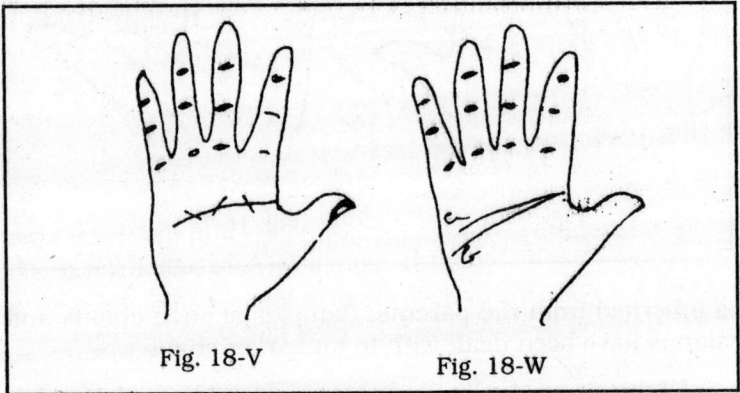

Fig. 18-V   Fig. 18-W

If there is no Head Line, it indicates lack of power of thought. If the Head Line is there but the Heart Line is missing, it indicates a cunning and miserly nature.

If there are two Head lines instead of one, given that the other signs are good, the person has many talents and a multifaceted personality. But if the other signs are bad, it indicates a person beset with indecisiveness. Two Head Lines might be parallel to each other or might run in different directions (*see Fig. 18-Wa, Wb*).

If the Head Line branches out as soon as it originates, with one of the branches going towards the Mount of Jupiter and the other touching the Life Line, it indicates good fortune from the very beginning of one's life (*see Fig. 18-X*).

If one of the branches of the Head Line goes towards the Heart Line (*see Fig. 18-Y*), the person is likely to surrender his mind to his feelings and sentiments. His power of reasoning is diminished. If the branch rises to merge with the Heart Line, it means that the person has stopped thinking and would act emotionally (*see Fig. 18-Z*). If the Mount of Venus and the Aggressive Mars are developed, the person has excessive sex drive.

Fig. 18-X   Fig. 18-Y   Fig. 18-Z

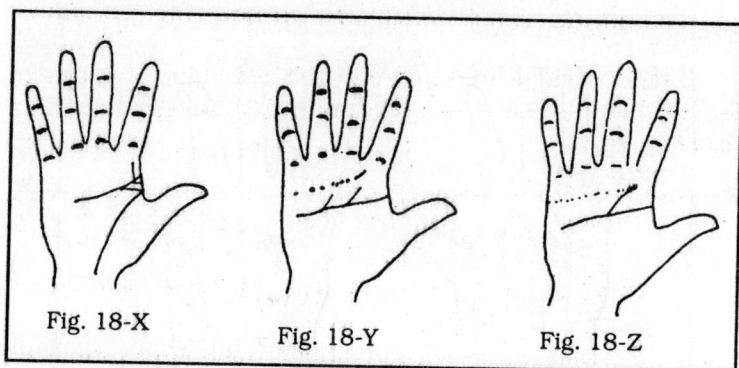

If the distance between the Head Line and the Heart Line is less (see Fig. 18-AA), the person is liable to hold fixed ideas. He has a tendency to resist his own ideas. If the distance is more, there is flexibility in his views (see Fig. 18-BB).

Fig. 18-AA   Fig. 18-BB

A wavy Head Line indicates moodiness in a person.

A broad, shallow Head Line indicates a state of tension in the person. A person with a thin, shallow Head Line is likely to be carried away by other people's arguments.

Branches of the Head Line going upwards (see Fig. 18-CC) indicate an optimistic frame of mind and conversely, those going downwards speak of a pessimistic disposition (see Fig. 18-DD).

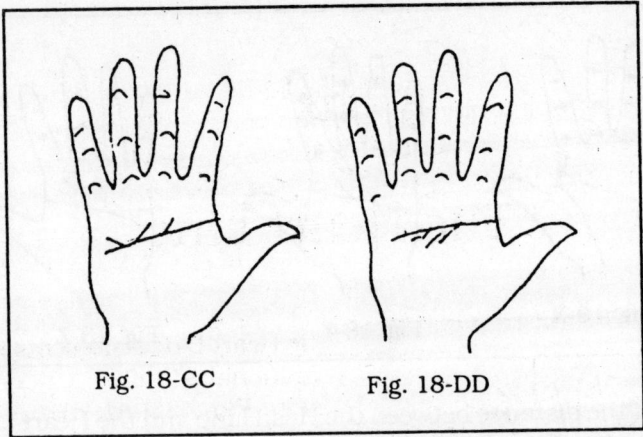

Fig. 18-CC   Fig. 18-DD

If the branches going upwards are in a large number, it indicates a tendency towards wasting one's mental energy.

A star at the end of a short Head Line is indicative of some form of mental disorder.

XIX

The Heart Line

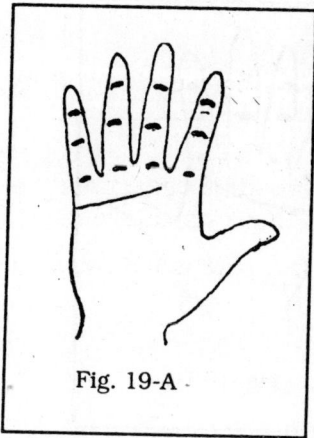

Fig. 19-A

The Heart Line represents the emotional state of a person (see Fig. 19-A). Human sentiments include love, sympathy, friendship, affection, jealousy, etc. Love, affection and friendship are positive sentiments, whereas jealousy and anger are negative in character. All the sentiments depend on how sensitive a person is and this is indicated by the Heart Line. It also is a mirror of the health of the organ, namely, the heart.

Western palmists are prone to read this line to answer questions about a person's love affairs and marriage, but the author's experience is that this line alone cannot answer these questions. One has to look for a cross on the Mount of Jupiter to know whether a person's desire for another of the opposite sex would be met. You have also to study other signs on the palm — the marriage line and indications about the sexuality of a person before you can answer any questions about his love relationships or the possibility of marriage. We shall come to these signs at their appropriate places.

Main Points of Origin of the Heart Line

- The third phalange of the index finger (see Fig. 19-Ba).

- The Mount of Jupiter *(see Fig. 19-Bb)*.

- The area lying between the first and the second fingers or the one lying between the Mounts of Jupiter and Saturn *(see Fig. 19-Bc)*.

- The Mount of Saturn under the middle finger *(See Fig. 19-Bd)*.

The point at which this line terminates lies between the Mount of Mercury and the Defensive Mars.

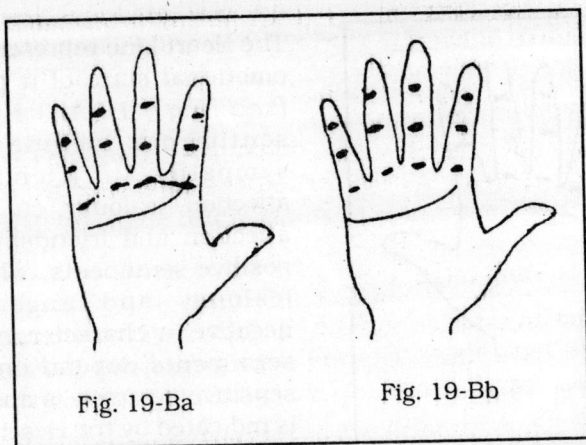

Fig. 19-Ba   Fig. 19-Bb

If the Heart Line is short, you can take it that the sentiments of that person would not be intense. An incomplete line indicates that a person is deficient in human sympathy, love and friendship. If the line is missing altogether, you can take it that the person is without any sentiments. We have already spoken of the Simian Line, a single horizontal line.

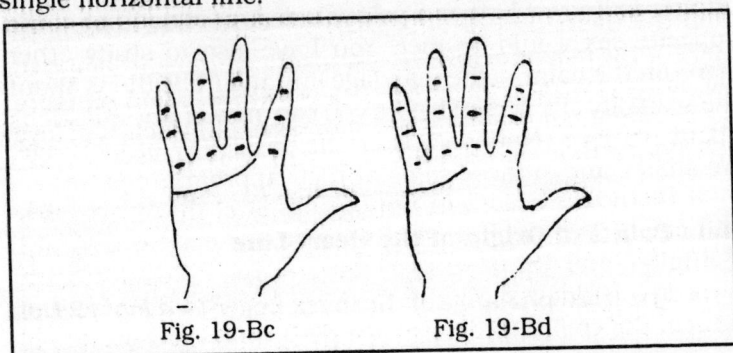

Fig. 19-Bc   Fig. 19-Bd

All the Secrets of Palmistry

If the Heart Line is deep and long, i.e. it touches the end of the palm and goes beyond the Mount of Jupiter, a person's love is more akin to worship than an affair of the heart. If he is disappointed in love, the person may become a victim of jealousy, enmity and even madness. Love, of course means, the feeling that the members of the opposite sex have for each other, but it also includes friendship. The line, must therefore, be taken to indicate both kinds of love.

A long Heart Line, which is thin but deep, is considered to be the best. Such persons have healthy hearts. They have the required amount of affection, love and human sympathy. If the line is wide and shallow, the emotions of the person may be either weak or strong.

If the line originates from the third phalange of the index finger the person is likely to be hypersensitive (see Fig. 19-Ba). If there is even the slightest doubt about the fidelity of the object of his love, the fires of jealousy start raging inside his breast and might even burn him out.

If the line starts from the Mount of Jupiter, the person is likely to have more goodwill than love. Such persons are always in search of ideal objects of their love giving secondary importance to the physical aspect of love. What they are looking for is a situation is which the love of the opposite party gives them mental satisfaction (see Fig. 19-Bb).

Persons whose Heart Line originates from a point between the Mounts of Jupiter and Saturn take a practical outlook in matters of affection. They do not expect much from the object of their love, nor do they get dejected if there is no response (see Fig. 19-Bc).

If the Heart Line originates from the base of the middle finger or the Mount of Saturn, the emotion of love and human sympathy is weak. The person is more likely to find pleasure in sexual relations without any corresponding feeling of love (see Fig. 19-Bd).

If there is a trident at the beginning of the Heart Line, with one of its branches going towards the middle of Mount of Jupiter and the Mount of Saturn, the second branch towards the index finger and the third towards the Mount of Saturn, the emotions of love, sympathy and the sexuality of a person are in balance *(see Fig. 19-C)*.

There is more of sentimentality if the line is semi-circular *(see Fig. 19-D)*, and less of it if the line is straight *(see Fig. 19-E)*.

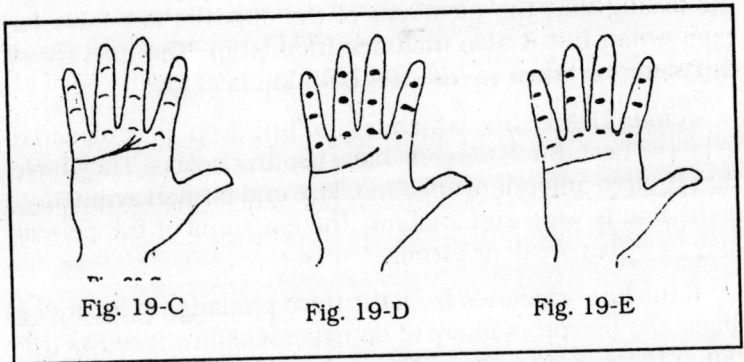

Fig. 19-C   Fig. 19-D   Fig. 19-E

If the line is broken or is full of chains, it indicates that emotional shocks afflict the heart of that person. The shocks may be due to lack of response from the object of his love or from somebody towards whom the person has feelings of affection. If there is a square on such a line, the person is able to bear such shocks.

A broken Heart Line indicates a broken heart, the reason being lack of response from the object of love or affection. If there is another line forming a bridge *(see Fig. 19-F)*, this fault gets diminished.

A Heart Line with an island on it indicates weakness of the heart caused by emotional attachment.

If along with a defective Heart Line, the Life Line is also defective, i.e. if the latter is broken or has an island over it, there might be heart disorders. The time at which these disorders will occur can be calculated according to the rule which applies to the Life Line, of which we have spoken earlier.

If the Heart Line originates from a point near the Head Line, the person is more practical than emotional in his mental makeup. There is a tendency to give second place to sentiments if they come in the way of his getting what he wants *(see Fig. 19-G).*

If the Heart Line runs close to the base of the fingers, the person is likely to be more sentimental *(see Fig. 19-H).*

The mount towards which the branches of the Heart Line tend to incline has effect on the emotional makeup of the person. If the branch goes towards the Mount of Jupiter, the person is likely to be a faithful friend. If it goes towards the Mount of Saturn, the person runs away from matrimonial relations and would like to restrict his relations towards the person of the opposite sex to a mere sexual alliance. If the branch goes towards the Mount of Apollo or Sun, the person is likely to take into consideration the social position of the opposite sex before deciding on marriage.

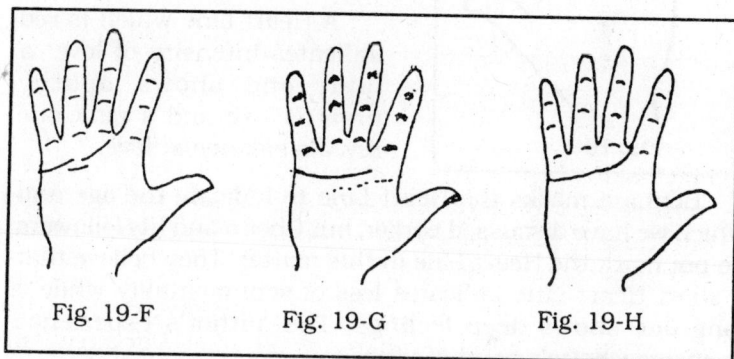

Fig. 19-F   Fig. 19-G   Fig. 19-H

Small lines that intersect the Heart Line indicate obstacles which come in the way of a person's love/affection finding a response and the tension that accompanies such matters. If the intersecting lines are deep, it indicates loss of health because of emotional troubles. If the Line of the Sun or the Line of Saturn intersects the Heart Line, it does not have negative effects which are associated with such intersection because the Heart Line comes between these vertical lines.

If you find a point, a cross, a star or an island on the Heart Line, consult the Life Line too before you make any predictions. If the Life Line is defective, a disorder of the heart is indicated, but if the Life Line is without any bad aspects, it indicates disappointment in love. If that is so, the Line of Mars and the one affecting a person's marriage/

sexuality should be studied, before offering a prognosis. Details on these lines are given at an appropriate place in this book.

If the first part of the Heart Line is without any defects, but defects show in the latter part, there are obstacles in the fulfilment of his love. If the concluding part of the line is good, the person is able to surmount these obstacles.

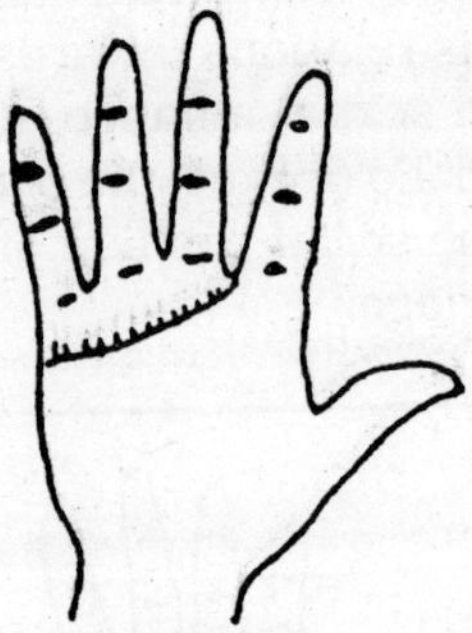

Fig. 19-I

If in the upper part of the line there are small lines resembling the teeth of a saw that incline upwards, there is no permanence in love (see Fig. 19-I).

A Heart Line which is red indicates intensity of love; a faint one shows apathy towards love and a pink one reveals balance in love.

Benham marks the Heart Line to indicate the age and which we have discussed earlier, but Cheiro and his followers do not mark the Heart Line in this matter. They believe that a short Heart Line indicates less of sentimentality while a long one shows deep feelings. The author's experience confirms Cheiro's point of view.

XX

Line of Saturn

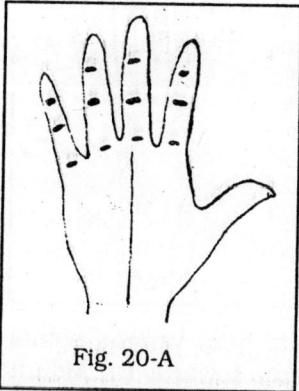

Fig. 20-A

Known as *Urdhvamukhi Rekha* (vertical line) or *Indira Rekha* in the *Samudrika Shastra*, the Line of Saturn is also called the Line of Fate or Wealth by some palmists *(see Fig. 20-A).* This line indicates the amount of money or property a person is likely to possess and also his prospects in business or employment, but as we have said earlier, Cheiro did not read only this line to find out the worldly possessions of a person; he also studied the Head Line to answer questions on this subject.

Most palmists believe that the Line of Saturn without the Line of Sun has no significance. The author agrees with this view to a great extent, because a person's luck depends on his health, his worldly possessions and the mental peace that he has. It is in view of this that we have chosen to call it the Line of Saturn, instead of the Line

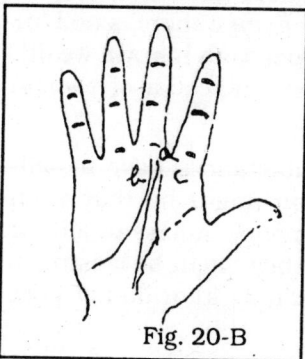

Fig. 20-B

of Fate or the Line of Wealth. It is so called because it goes towards the Mount of Saturn.

The Line of Saturn originates from the following points:

• The wrist *(see Fig. 20-Ba).*

• The Mount of Moon *(see Fig. 20-Bb).*

• The Life Line *(see Fig. 20-Bc).*

- The Mount of Venus *(see Fig. 20-Ca)*.

The Line of Saturn sometimes originates from the middle of the palm or the Plain of Mars or the Head Line *(see Fig. 20-Cb)* or the Heart Line *(see Fig. 20-Cc)*. No matter from where it originates, it ends at the Mount of Saturn.

Sometimes the line does not reach the Mount of Saturn but ends on the way. Because it heads towards the Mount of Saturn, it is called the Line of Saturn *(see Fig. 20-D)*.

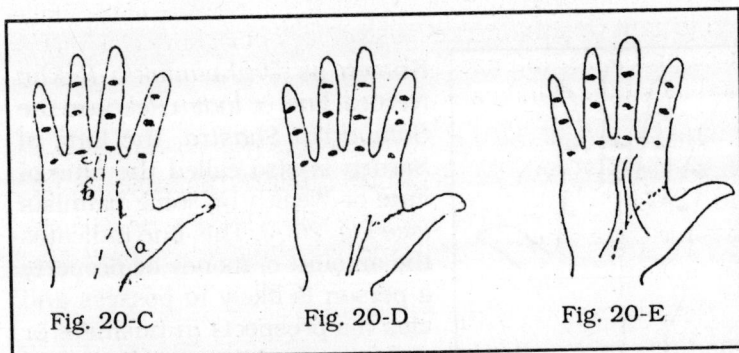

Fig. 20-C   Fig. 20-D   Fig. 20-E

In some palms the lines originate from various points and run parallel to each other to march towards the Mount of Saturn *(see Fig. 20-E)*.

Is it the Line of Fate?

You must have come across many wealthy persons whose palms are devoid of the Line of Saturn and many poor persons who have a well-defined Line of Saturn. There are reasons for this, some of which are mentioned here. A person born in a rich family inherits wealth and does not have to put in any mental or physical labour for it. Even if there is no Line of Saturn, he is rich. But if a person destroys his own wealth or multiplies it through his efforts, some indication of it would be available in the Line of Saturn.

Many persons in adverse circumstances have a well-defined Line of Saturn. The reason might be that such persons exert their minds to earn money, amass wealth or simply to earn their livelihood, but they might be lacking in money for investing (in order to multiply it) or do not have

All the Secrets of Palmistry

the proper environment in which they can succeed. The line is found in the palms of those persons too who have money and who are constantly trying to multiply it. One must, therefore, study a person's Line of Sun too to predict his fate, because the Line of Saturn alone does not represent a person's fortune, good or bad.

A defective Line of Saturn is indicative of the fact that a person is making endeavours all the time to earn money and to gain wealth, but because of lack of right decisions he faces problems. Intense desire for wealth, a weak desire or total lack of it is indicated by this line.

The question arises that if desire is the deciding factor, what role does fate play in man's affairs? The only way we can answer this question is to point out that fate is an invisible force which gives a man the ambition to rise in the world.

Nobody has seen the hands which manufactured the computer and which is called the human brain of a machine. The computer has its own place, but the 'remote control' which runs it is our mind. Who runs the mind? Call it the soul, the Supreme Soul or God, or the actions of a person's previous incarnation. Faith alone answers these questions according to one's own beliefs.

We cannot see these invisible forces, but can try to read the language of the lines on the palm.

The author had the opportunity to study the lines of the palms of some infants and he found the Line of Saturn in some of them. The question now arises: How does that infant understand the importance of money or wealth or employment or for that matter and how can he exert himself in that direction?

A good deal of study and thought has provided some of the answers.

The Hindus believe that a person's life is determined by his actions in a previous life, but scientists say that it is the chromosomes and genes, which a person inherits from his parents, that play a dominant role in making a person what he is. Chromosomes and genes are supposed to be the foundation on which a person's character is based. But, whether it is the actions of a previous life or the chromosomes and genes, the possibilities which are hidden in a person make their appearance at a proper time. And when they do, they are clearly in evidence for all to see. A person who can gauge the hidden possibilities before they appear is a specialist, so to speak, and a palmist is a specialist in that sense.

And now we come to the method of reading the graph which the Line of Saturn represents.

If the Line of Saturn emanates from the wrist and goes to the Mount of Saturn without touching the Life Line, it indicates a condition in which there are no fluctuations in a person's financial status. Such a person has a clear and definite goal in life (see Fig. 20-A).

If this line emanates from the Mount of Moon, it indicates a desire for worldly goods and also the aspiration to be

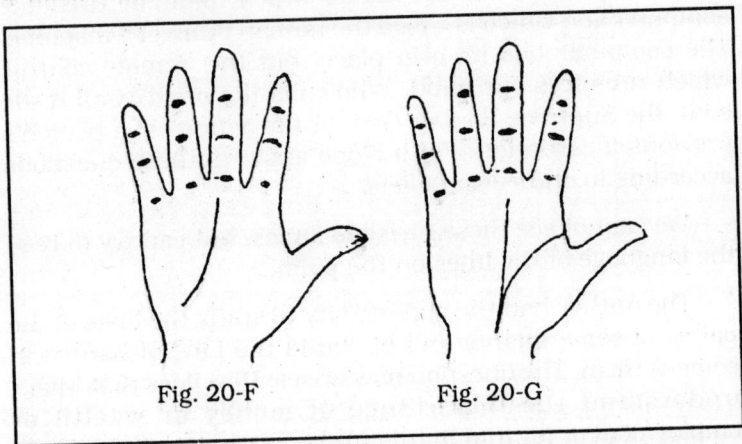

Fig. 20-F   Fig. 20-G

accepted by one's peers. In other words, such a person would not use unfair means to gain wealth (see Fig. 20-F). If such a line is deep and clear, the person's desires will be fulfilled.

If the origin of the Line of Saturn is as a single line merging with the Life Line and separating later to move towards the Mount of Saturn (see Fig. 20-G), it means that the man's fate in the earlier part of his life is bound with his family. His identity as an individual would manifest itself

All the Secrets of Palmistry

only when the line separates from the Life Line to go towards the Mount of Saturn. At that point of time in his life he may work independently or open new branches of a business run by his family and show some progress on his own. Questions regarding physical health pertaining to the period represented by that part of the line which is one with the Life Line can be answered by calculating his age from the Life Line. Questions regarding his career can be answered according to the rule concerning calculation of age from the Line of Saturn.

If the Line of Saturn starts from the Mount of Venus or from below the Life Line (see Fig. 20-H), it indicates that the person was burdened with family responsibilities in the earlier part of his life. When the line intersects the Life Line and goes towards the Mount of Saturn, the person is free from family responsibilities and tries to find his own way in the world.

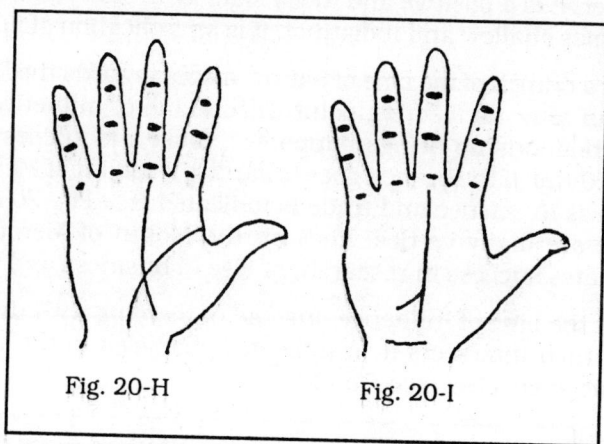

Fig. 20-H   Fig. 20-I

If a Line of Influence emanating from the Mount of Moon meets the Line of Saturn, it indicates that at that point of time in his life the person would meet an individual who would be instrumental in his progress. Such a line can also be an indication of marriage or love (see Fig. 20-I). If the Line of Influence originating from the Mount of Moon runs with the Line of Saturn, it is an indication of his association with a wealthy family. The time at which this is possible can be calculated according to the rule applied to calculate age from the Line of Saturn (see Fig. 20-J).

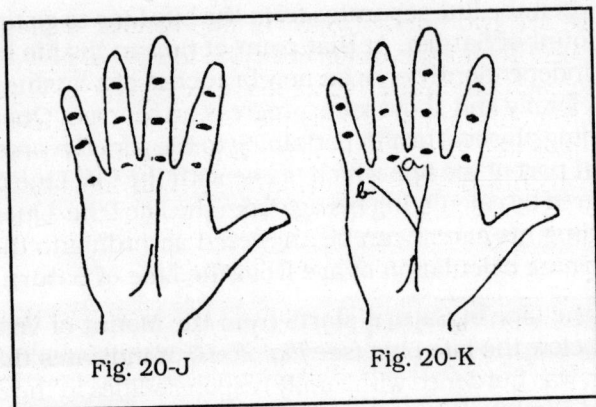

Fig. 20-J   Fig. 20-K

If after meeting the Line of Influence coming from the Mount of Moon, the Line of Saturn becomes deeper and clearer, it is a positive and lucky sign. Conversely, if the line becomes shallow and indistinct, it is an indication of ill luck.

If a branch of the Line of Saturn moves towards the Mount of Sun after its meeting point with a Line of Influence, the new relationship brings happiness, fame and success (see Fig. 20-Ka). If the branch goes towards the Mount of Mercury, success in science and trade is indicated (see Fig. 20-Kb). If there are many vertical lines on the Mount of Mercury, it indicates success in research, or else in business and trade.

If the Line of Influence, instead of merging with the Line of Saturn intersects it, it indicates obstacles in the way of financial success (see Fig. 20-L).

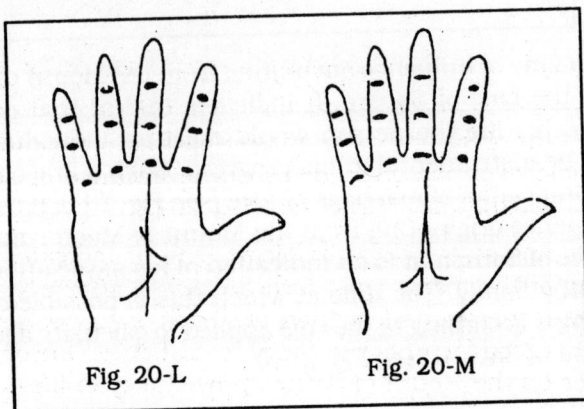

Fig. 20-L   Fig. 20-M

If there are two lines of Saturn, one coming from the Mount of Venus and the other from the Mount of Moon to merge into each other after some distance, the person gets help both from his family and people outside the confines of his home (see Fig. 20-M). If both the lines move separately, then one which is deeper has more effect than the other.

A Line of Saturn emanating from the Plain of Mars indicates good fortune during youth (see Fig. 20-N).

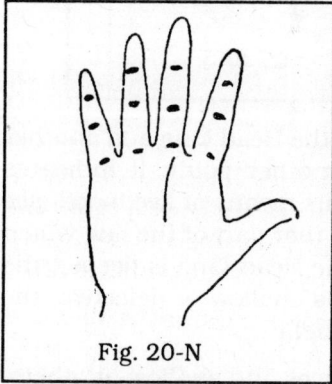

Fig. 20-N

If the Line of Saturn starts from the Head Line, it is an indication of the person laying the foundation of his fortune during youth because of a wise decision taken by him (see Fig. 20-O). But if the line stops at the Head Line (see Fig. 20-P), it indicates an obstacle in the person's good fortune, because of a wrong decision on his part.

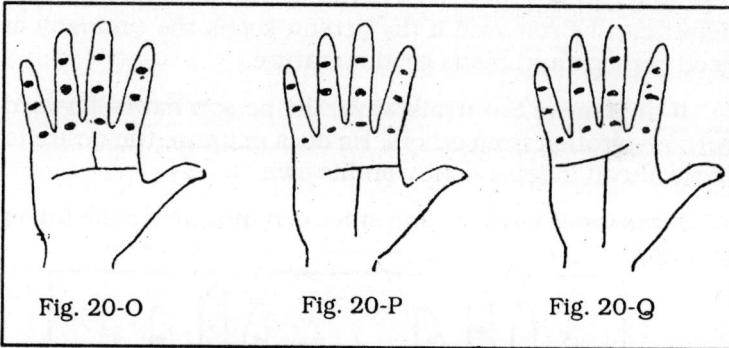

Fig. 20-O   Fig. 20-P   Fig. 20-Q

If the Line of Saturn stops at the Heart Line, it indicates an obstacle to a person's good fortune because of some impulsive action taken earlier (see Fig. 20-Q).

If this line starts from the Heart Line, it indicates the beginning of the man's good fortune during later age (see Fig. 20-R). If there are more than two lines on the Mount of Saturn, his good fortune is not very remarkable. One or two such lines on the Mount of Saturn prove lucky in life.

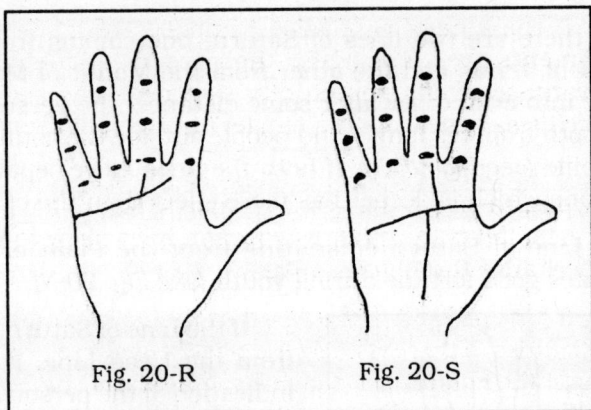

Fig. 20-R   Fig. 20-S

If the Line of Saturn stops at the Head Line and another Line of Saturn emerges from another point, it indicates changes in a person's career or his means of livelihood (see Fig. 20-S). But, one has to notice that part of the line which is deeper. If the segment after the Head Line is deeper, the change is lucky, but if the part is shallow or defective, the change would be without any benefit.

If the line is deep at some places and shallow at others, a person can face problems because of indecisiveness. This defect can be removed if the person keeps the company of good persons and reads good literature.

If the Line of Saturn is wavy, the person moves forward with inspiration from others. He does not have the desire to move ahead independently on his own.

A wide and shallow Line of Saturn indicates a life full of struggle.

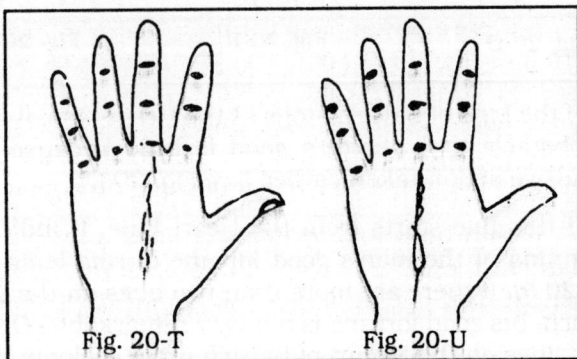

Fig. 20-T   Fig. 20-U

If the Line of Saturn is composed of many pieces or segments *(see Fig. 21-T)*, the person is unable to take advantage of any opportunity that come his way. It gives much less benefit than a single, unbroken line does.

If the Line of Saturn is better in the active hand than in the passive hand, the person is able to add to the patrimony he gets. If it is the other way round, he is likely to waste the inheritance through its misuse.

A Line of Saturn composed of chains indicates financial difficulties. If there is an island on it, it signifies loss of wealth where the chains occur *(see Fig. 20-U)*.

If the island is on the point where a Line of Influence from the Mount of Moon meets the Line of Saturn, there is likelihood of harm being caused due to marriage or from one's partner *(see Fig. 20-V)*.

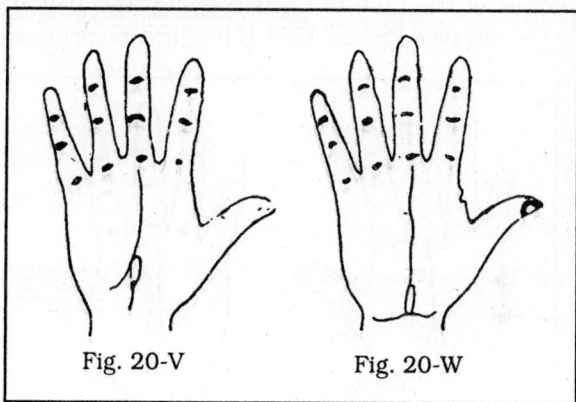

Fig. 20-V   Fig. 20-W

If there are islands in the beginning of the line, problems are indicated because of the circumstances of the parents *(see Fig. 20-W)*. If the line improves later on, financial troubles get removed. Some palmists interpret the presence of islands in the beginning of the line as a possibility of death of parents in early life or the possibility of being an adopted child.

If thin horizontal or oblique lines intersect the Line of Saturn, there are obstacles to a person attaining financial benefit. But one must see the mount from which the lines

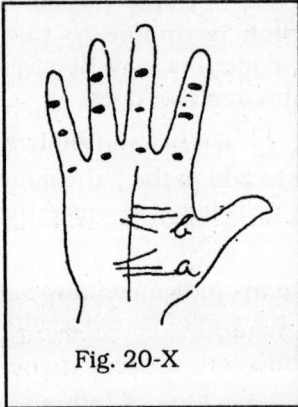

Fig. 20-X

emanate. If they come from the Mount of Venus, obstacles are created by a person of the opposite sex from the family *(see Fig. 20-Xa)*. If they originate from any place in the Aggressive Mars, the obstacles are created by a member of the family from the same sex *(see Fig. 20-Xb)*. If the lines coming from these mounts stop short of the Line of Saturn, the obstacles are removed. But if the line becomes faint after its intersection with such lines, then obstacles become difficult to solve. If further on, the line remains distinct, the obstacles get removed.

Branches of the Line of Saturn going upwards indicate financial benefit *(see Fig. 21-Yab)*. If the branches are inclined

Fig. 20-Y   Fig. 20-Z

downwards, it indicates financial difficulties at that age *(see Fig. 21-Ycd)*. But one must ensure that the lines going downward are not really lines coming from the Mount of Luna or Mount of Venus but merging with the Line of Saturn.

Lines which merge into the Line of Saturn indicate good or bad influence. If after the merger, the line becomes clear, it is a sign of good luck; conversely, if it becomes faint, ill luck is indicated.

All the Secrets of Palmistry

If subsidiary lines move with a weak Line of Saturn, its negative aspects are rectified *(see Fig. 20-Z)*.

If the line stops short of the Mount of Saturn, it indicates that financial resources of the person would decrease when he reaches old age. If it is caused by ill health and the Life Line would indicate it.

The Line of Saturn also indicates life's struggles and the fluctuations in one's fortune.

If the line is non-existent, it is a sign of lack of ambition on the part of the person for either money or employment. He is satisfied with what he has and there are not many obstacles in his life.

Significance of the Line of Saturn on a Housewife's Palm

The Line of Saturn is found on the palms of women who do not engage in any trade and do not take up any employment. The line in their case signifies a desire on their part to have more money. If financial resources are limited, they would save and keep their money intact. If a housewife has a good Line of Sun in addition to the Line of Saturn, then her husband is lucky financially. Another consequence of a good Line of Sun is that she will have a wide circle of friends and acquaintances.

XXI

Line of Sun

Hindu palmistry in *Samudrika Shastra* calls this line as the *Dharma Rekha* (Line of Religion), the *Punya Rekha* (Line of Spiritual Gain) and the *Saraswati Rekha* or the *Vidya Rekha* (Line of Knowledge) *(see Fig. 21-A)*. Western palmists designate it as the Line of Sun or Apollo. It ends at the Mount of Sun and hence the nomenclature. This line is a mirror of the success of a person's endeavours.

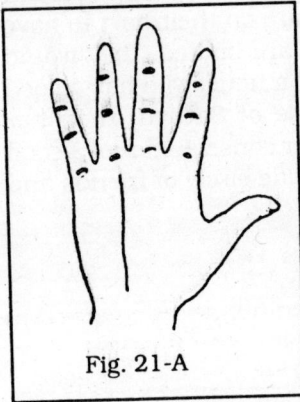

Fig. 21-A

Success has many faces: for a student, it means success in an examination; for a businessman it lies in furthering his business, and for a litigant it means victory in a case. A man in employment measures his success by the promotion that he gets and a politician by his rising to a position of power. The position of the line must, therefore, be interpreted according to the field in which a person is active.

Some palmists try to find the answers to wealth and employment in the Line of Saturn. Cheiro believed that the Head Line should also be studied, but I would also like to see the Line of Sun because it is a supporting line of the Line of Saturn.

The Line of Saturn indicates the quantity of worldly goods a person is likely to possess, but, if the Line of Sun is positive, efforts made by the person to gain wealth are likely to succeed. Without a positive Line of Sun, the result is always in doubt.

All the Secrets of Palmistry

Saturn represents qualities like sobriety, stability, wisdom and sadness, whereas the Sun represents intensity which is visible. Love for solitude by a person with a prominent Saturn impels him to work single-mindedly towards the attainment of his objective, but if his Line of Sun is not helpful, his good work does not reach the people and fails to produce desirable results. If the Line of Sun is helpful, the person will succeed in his endeavours.

The number of palms in which the Line of Saturn is present but the Line of Sun is missing are many, but the number of palms with the Sun Line but no Line of Saturn, is limited. A Line of Sun without a Line of Saturn indicates success in all spheres except wealth and worldly goods. The spheres could be education, public life or just court cases.

It must be made clear that the vertical lines on the Mount of Sun should not be confused with the line itself; in fact, such lines are Lines of Influence which start showing their effect after the age of 56.

If the ring finger is long and the Sun Line is good, the person succeeds in adventure. If the Line of Saturn is also good, adventurous activities remain within control. He succeeds in his ventures and also accumulates wealth. But if the Line of Saturn is there but the Line of Sun is missing, the person will not be happy even if all the good things of life are available. He will always feel insecure.

One must see the Line of Sun in addition to the Line of Saturn while answering questions about the amount of wealth. If you want to know whether a person would succeed in arts, look at the Mount of Moon too. For questions relating to trade and politics, the Mounts of Mercury and Sun should be studied.

To sum up, the Line of Sun tends to strengthen the good effects of the various other lines; it also reduces their negative aspects if it is good.

The points of origin of the Line of Sun are

- Wrist (see Fig. 21-Ba).

- Mount of Moon (see Fig. 21-Bb).

- Line of Saturn *(see Fig. 21-Bc).*

- Life Line *(see Fig. 21-Bd).*

- The middle part of the palm, the Head Line or the Heart Line might also be the points of origin for the Sun Line.

The Line of Sun is so-called because it inclines towards the Mount of Sun.

Rare is a case where the Line of Sun starts from the wrist. In such a case, success is indicated from the very childhood. If it starts from the middle of the palm, success starts at the age indicated from its point of origin. Age in this case, should be calculated from the Line of Saturn, as indicated in Chapter XV.

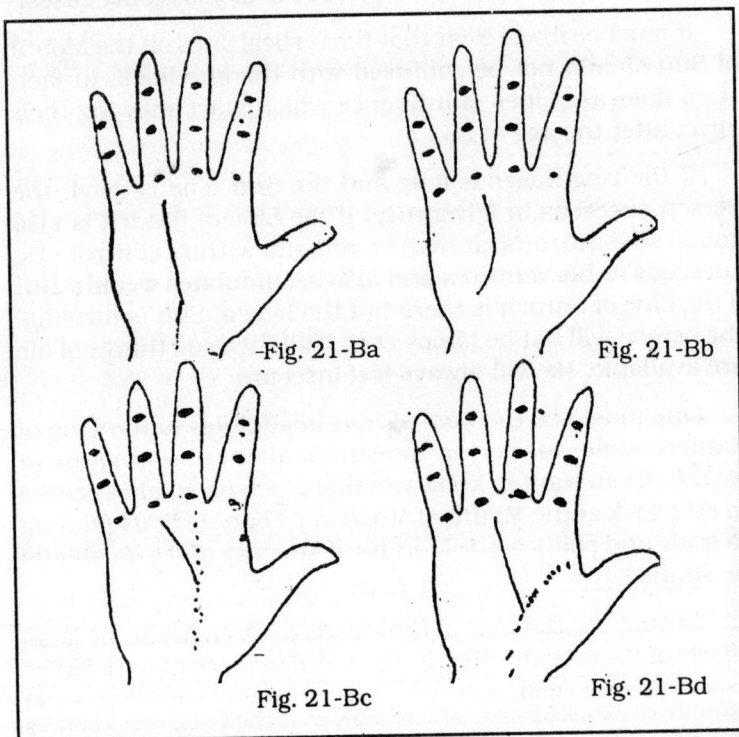

-Fig. 21-Ba

Fig. 21-Bb

Fig. 21-Bc

Fig. 21-Bd

If the ring finger of a person whose Line of Sun starts from the wrist is long, he has a tendency to undertake risky ventures. A long thumb tends to weaken this tendency, but a short thumb with a long ring finger tends to intensify this tendency.

A person whose Line of Sun originates from the Mount of Moon succeeds with the cooperation and help from others, some of whom might belong to another country (see Fig. 21-Bb).

If a Line of Sun emanates from the Line of Saturn as its branch moves towards the Mount of Sun, it indicates success in making money, in employment or in business (see Fig. 21-Bc). If alongwith this, the Mount of Moon is also prominent, it indicates financial benefits from fine arts.

A Line of Sun emanating from the Life Line as its branch indicates success through a person's own endeavours and ability (see Fig. 21-Bd). The age at which success would come can be calculated from the Line of Saturn.

A Line of Sun emanating from the middle of the palm indicates success in youth (see Fig. 21-C). If it emanates from the Defensive Mars, it shows that the person is an able public speaker who gains fame for his oratory (see Fig. 21-D).

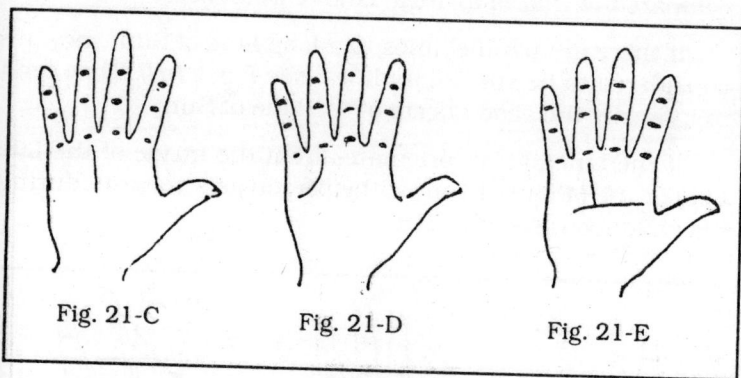

Fig. 21-C   Fig. 21-D   Fig. 21-E

If the Line of Sun originates from the Head Line, it is indicative of success at the age of 35. Such success is achieved in the fields of philosophy, mathematics or science because of the inherent ability of a person (see Fig. 21-E) in such subjects.

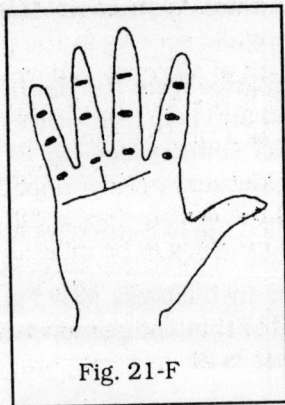
Fig. 21-F

If the Line of Sun arises as a branch of the Heart Line, it is an indication of a successful marriage *(see Fig. 21-F)*. Such a line must be distinguished from vertical lines on the Mount of Sun. The time at which the marriage will take place can be calculated from other signs. While doing this, try to study the period on the Line of Saturn when it was a good sign. If there are no indications on the Mount of Saturn, see the Mount of Jupiter for a cross near the Life Line. The marriage would be happy and would take place early. If there is no such sign, it can be assumed that the marriage would be a happy one.

Vertical lines on the Mount of the Sun indicate success after the age of 55. One or two such lines are considered auspicious *(see Fig. 21-G)*. More than two such lines indicate lack of concentration in one's efforts because the person might have too many irons in the fire. Their effect is less as compared to that of a single Line of Influence.

If there are parallel lines to a long Line of Sun, they are considered to be subsidiary lines *(see Fig. 21-H)*. They tend to intensify the good effects of the Line of Sun.

If the Line of Sun originates from the inside of the Life Line or the Mount of Venus, the person gets security during his childhood *(see Fig. 21-I)*.

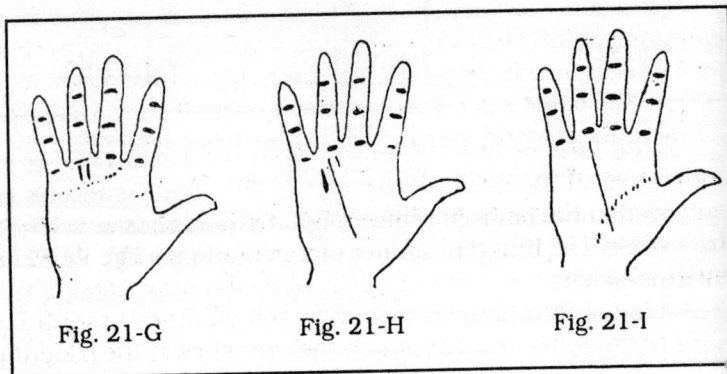
Fig. 21-G   Fig. 21-H   Fig. 21-I

All the Secrets of Palmistry

If the Line of Sun is good and the Aggressive Mars well developed, the person gets fame while serving in the police, the army or in sports. If the Mount of Mercury is developed, it indicates fame in politics and if the Mount of Saturn is developed, the person succeeds as a philosopher.

If the Mounts of Saturn and Mercury are developed, but the little finger is twisted, the Line of Sun has a different significance. Such a person is more likely to be infamous for his anti-social activities.

A broken Line of Sun indicates that the person is not a specialist in any field. His success is always temporary.

A double Line of Sun indicates success in many fields.

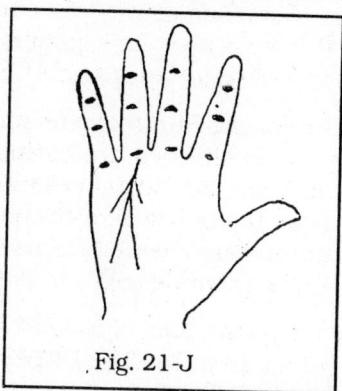

Fig. 21-J

If the lines emanating from various places merge into one to become the Line of Sun, the person achieves success in many fields because of his multifarious talents (see Fig. 21-J).

If there is no Line of Sun, the person does not gain fame in spite of his efforts and talents that he possesses.

If there is an island or a cross on the Line of Sun, it indicates a blemish on the person's reputation. But a star tends to add to a person's fame.

Transverse lines intersecting the Line of Sun indicate obstacles to success and fame. If the lines arise from the Mount of Mercury, obstacles are created by rivals or colleagues. If they emanate from Aggressive Mars, a person of the same sex creates obstacles and if they arise from the Mount of Moon, persons from fine arts such create obstacles in the path of success of a person.

If horizontal lines intersect the Line of Sun at the Mount of Sun, it brings infamy in later life. A square saves a man from harm. If there is a trident at the upper end of the Sun Line of Sun, fame comes from the qualities associated with the mounts towards which the branches of the trident point.

If the fingers are pointed or rounded when the Line of Sun is good, it indicates success in arts. Spatulate fingers bring fame in matters which are practical. Knotty fingers bring fame in mathematics, philosophy and other intellectual endeavours.

Persons without a Line of Sun are also found to succeed in life, but their success is not due to their own efforts but because of the help they get from their family and friends.

XXII

Line of Mercury

Palmists disagree on the Line of Mercury *(see Fig. 22-A)* which we will discuss and will outline our own conclusions about the significance of the line.

The *Samudrika Shastra* calls the Line of Mercury the *Swasthya Rekha* (the Line of Health). Western palmists call it the Line of Health or the Hepatica (Line of Liver) but according to this author's experience, this line tells more about success in a career or business than health.

The Life Line is a better indicator of health than this line and it is a misnomer to call it the Line of Health.

A point on which there is disagreement among the palmists is whether the Mount of Mercury is the point of origin or the point of termination of this line. Cheiro thought that this line started from Mount of Mercury and ended at the wrist or the Life Line or the Mount of Venus. He was also of the view that the point at which this line intersected the Life Line conveyed the time at which the person's life ended or it was a time of some grave crisis *(see Fig. 22-B)*.

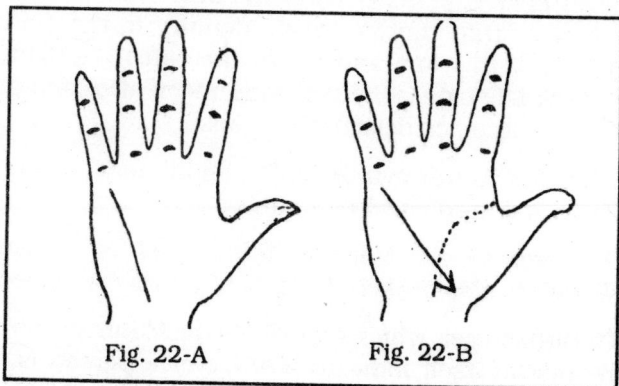

Fig. 22-A   Fig. 22-B

Desbarrolles, Benham and many other Western palmists believe that the line starts from the Mount of Moon or the wrist or the Life Line or the Mount of Venus and ends at the Mount of Mercury. The author agrees with their conclusion.

Most palmists believe that if the Line of Mercury starts from either the wrist or the Mount of Moon, or is distinct and deep, does not touch the Life Line and reaches the Mount of Mercury *(see Fig. 22-C)*, it is a good line; but if it is broken, it is bad.

If the Line of Mercury emanates from the Mount of Venus, and cuts the Life Line to reach the Mount of Mercury, it indicates that the person will progress during that period when the Line of Mercury crosses the Life Line. *(see Fig. 22D)*

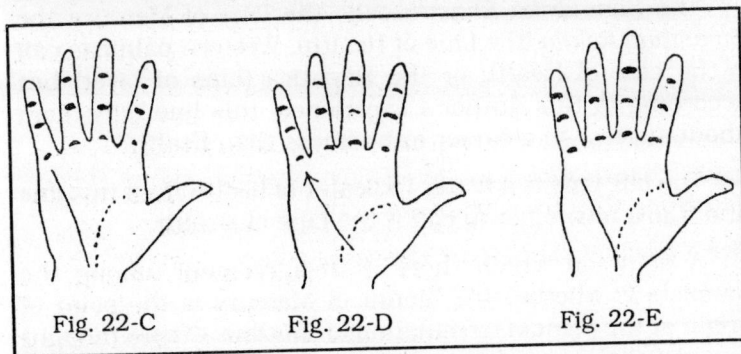

Fig. 22-C   Fig. 22-D   Fig. 22-E

The effect of the Line of Mercury emanating from the Life Line as a branch is the same as that of the one emanating from the Mount of Venus *(see Fig. 22-E)*.

The author's experience confirms this. There is truth in the statement that the Mount of Mercury is the point of termination of this line and is not the point of origin. Its touching the Life Line is inauspicious only if after that point the Life Line becomes defective or vanishes altogether.

The author has drawn the following inferences from his experience and studies on this subject:

• A broken Line of Mercury indicates ill health. And if the Life Line is also broken, then ill-health is confirmed.

• The little finger, which represents the Mount of Mercury and the mount itself indicate how clever a person is. The

All the Secrets of Palmistry

Mount of Mercury also indicates business acumen or the ability to study science or engage in research. All these things point to the possibility of the Mount of Mercury being connected to the central nervous system. From this point of view, the function of this line is similar to that of the Head Line. Even so, there is a difference between these two lines. The difference lies in the fact that the Head Line represents the whole brain. The finger which represents it on the palm is the thumb. The Line of Mercury, on the other hand, represents only that part of the brain which deals with matters of profit and loss and is judged by the little finger. The reason why it is called the Line of Health or the Line of Liver is that a person given to using his brain most of the time does not do any physical labour and as such it leads to disorders of the digestive system. The digestive system, as is well known, is directly connected with the liver. It is because of such secondary reasons that the Line of Mercury has been considered the Line of Health or the Line of Liver.

• In order to answer questions about health, the Life Line, the Heart Line, and the Mount of Moon should be studied along with the Line of Mercury.

The following, in brief, are the conclusions drawn by the author by studying this line.

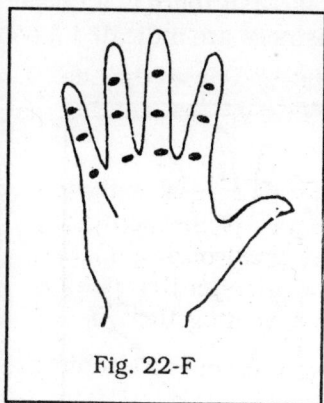

Fig. 22-F

• If the Line of Mercury starts from the middle of the palm and goes towards the Mount of Mercury (see Fig. 22-F), it signifies business acumen and inclination towards research.

• If the Line of Mercury starts from the Mount of Moon and is well-defined, it indicates an excellent health for the individual. If it is shallow, wide or broken, it indicates ailments of the digestive system or liver.

• If this line has islands over it, it might be an indication of a disease of the lungs (see Fig. 22-G) but if it is wavy, diseases like jaundice might afflict the person *(see Fig. 22-H)*. A line with chains on it signifies disorders of the stomach and liver.

If the line is composed of rungs of the ladder, it is indicative of disorders of the stomach, like flatulence *(see Fig. 22-I)*. If it is reddish in colour, a person would suffer from frequent fever.

Fig. 22-G   Fig. 22-H   Fig. 22-I

The author's experience reveals that a good, well-defined Line of Mercury indicates business and political acumen. If the line is defective, there is loss in business or profession. Its vertical branch or branches indicate profitable returns in business or profession *(see Fig. 22-J)*. If there is a tassle at the end of this line, losses in business are indicated *(see Fig. 22-K)*.

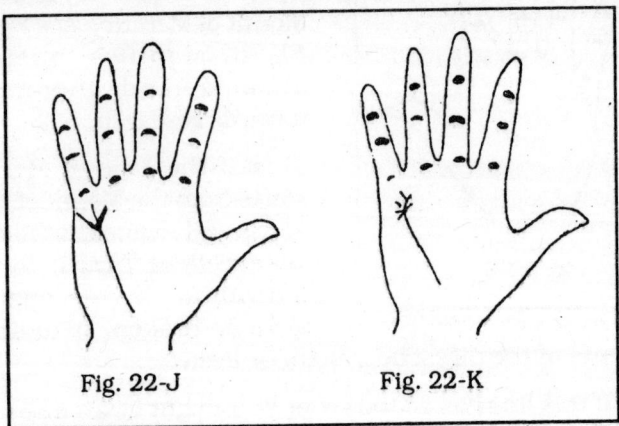

Fig. 22-J   Fig. 22-K

     All the Secrets of Palmistry

If the Line of Mercury rises from the wrist or if the Mount of Moon is well-defined and single, it is a measure of a person's clear-headedness. But a defective line, conversely, indicates mental confusion.

If there is no Line of Mercury on a person's palm, it is evidence of a carefree disposition. Such a person does not worry about anything and is, therefore, generally healthy.

XXIII

Marriage Lines/Lines of Sexuality

When palmists answer questions about marriage, most of them look at the horizontal lines on the outer edge of the Mount of Mercury, taking them to be Lines of Marriage (see Fig. 23-A). They count these lines and say that the number of marriages or love affairs would be equal to the number of these lines.

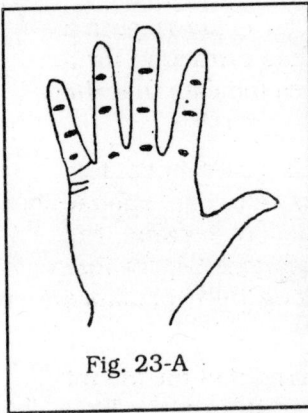

Fig. 23-A

In European countries where sexual relations before marriage are the general rule, these lines are also called Lines of Association or Lines of Affection.

One is reminded of an interesting incident. An acquaintance of this author bought a book on palmistry and when he saw two marriage lines on his wife's palm, he suspected that she had a secret love affair. It is because of such misinterpretation of lines that palmists in India call the shorter line as the Line of Engagement and the longer one as the Line of Marriage.

The author's experience and study tells him that these lines indicate less about marriage but more about the sexuality of a person. That is why he has called it the Line of Sexuality. If one wants to find something about marriage, then the other lines on the palm must also be studied in addition to these so-called Lines of Marriage.

The firmness or prominence of the Mount of Venus indicates the amount of sexuality a person possesses. But the Mount of Venus also indicates the amount of sympathy or vital force a person has. These lines near the Mount of Mercury actually indicate sexuality. That is why I have chosen to call them the Lines of Sexuality.

Line of Marriage

This is a horizontal line which enters the palm from the extreme percussion edge of the hand. That is why one must make a note of its position while taking a handprint (see Fig. 23-A). It starts from the edge of the palm and ends at the Mount of Mercury.

A line reaching the middle of the Mount of Mercury is a normal one; if it stops short of that point, it is short and if it goes beyond that point, it is considered to be long. If it reaches near the Mount of Sun, it is very long.

This author believes that one single Line of Marriage in a palm merely indicates that the person has attraction for a person of the opposite sex. Two such lines indicate that the sexuality would endure for a long time.

If such a line or lines are straight and well-defined, it is indicative of the fact that the person loves his spouse passionately. If there is no such line on a palm, the prominence of the Mount of Venus tends to make up for that deficiency. A thick little finger with a long third phalange has a similar effect.

If there is no Line of Sexuality on a hand and the Mount of Venus is also levelled (or underdeveloped), with the little finger being short and thin, there is likelihood of that person possessing less of sexual urge. If the line is there but is indistinct, then there is lack of interest in marriage or sexual relations. If the Mount of Moon is prominent, then the lack of interest is accentuated.

If the first part of the line is deep and the last one shallow, the person loses interest in love, but conversely, if the line is shallow in the beginning and becomes deeper thereafter, love tends to become more intense. Please note 'percussion' is the beginning point.

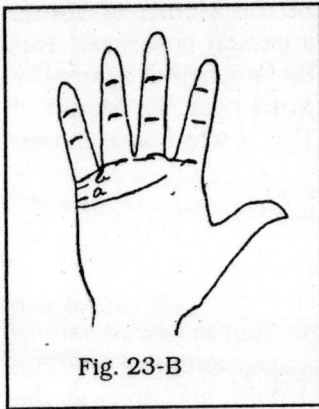

Fig. 23-B

If the Line of Sexuality is near the Heart Line (*see Fig. 23-Ba*), it is an indication, according to some palmists, of early marriage. But the author interprets such a line as indicative of sexuality becoming strong during adolescence. If the line is near the base of the little finger (*see Fig. 23-Bb*), the physical potential tends to increase after middle age.

If there is a single Line of Sexuality and lies halfway between the base of the little finger and the Heart Line, sexuality tends to be strong during youth. If the age at which marriage will take place is to be calculated, both the Mount of Jupiter and the Line of Saturn should be studied. If there is a cross on the Mount of Jupiter, near the Life Line, an early marriage is indicated. Elsewhere, a cross on the Mount of Jupiter indicates a happy marriage. If the Mount of Saturn is prominent, the marriage is delayed.

Early and late are relative terms and must be interpreted according to the society in which an individual lives. In India it is customary for a girl to get married at about 20 years of age but in the West, girls do not think of marriage before they are 25; in some cases, even 30. A marriage is late or early according to the customs prevalent in a region.

If there are two Lines of Sexuality, one near the base of the little finger and the other near the Heart Line, it signifies that sexuality, manifesting itself during adolescence, would continue even after middle age.

Benham measures the distance between the Heart Line and the base of the little finger as 70 years of age. He considers the middle point in this distance as signifying the age of 35 (*see Fig. 23-C*). But Marcel Broekman says that the space between the base of the little finger and the Heart Line signifies the age of 50 years. Half of that distance means 25 years (*see Fig. 23-D*). The author has found that Broekman is right to some extent.

All the Secrets of Palmistry

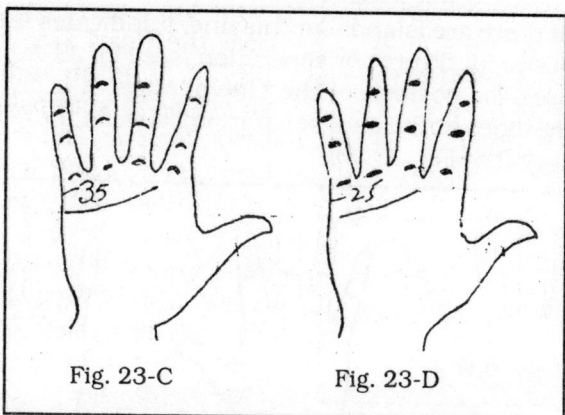

Fig. 23-C   Fig. 23-D

The author has reached the following conclusions about the Lines of Sexuality.

If the Line of Sexuality is inclined towards the Heart Line, it indicates ill health of the spouse (see Fig. 23-E). If the line so inclined intersects the Heart Line, death of the spouse (see Fig. 23-F) may take place.

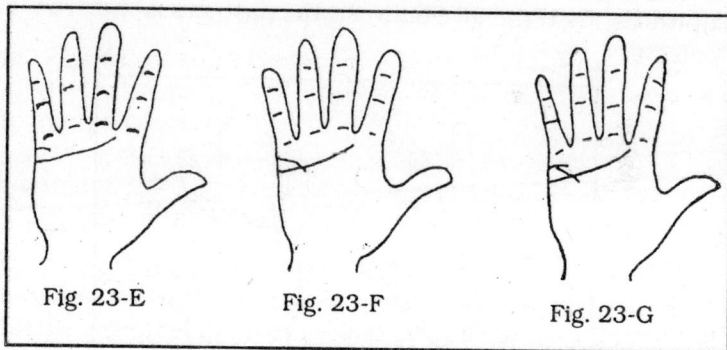

Fig. 23-E   Fig. 23-F   Fig. 23-G

• If the Line of Sexuality does not intersect the Heart Line but a branch of it does, it indicates marital troubles (see Fig. 23-G).

• If there is a break in the Line of Sexuality, there is a tendency to live away from one's spouse (see Fig. 23-H).

• If the Line of Sexuality is inclined towards the little finger, the spouse of that person is liable to outlive him/her (see Fig. 23-I).

• If there are islands on this line, it indicates tension, ill will, desire for divorce or separation (see Fig. 23-Ja). But one must see the position of the Line of Mars. If it divides into two branches at the end, separation between the couple is a certainty (see Fig. 23-Jb).

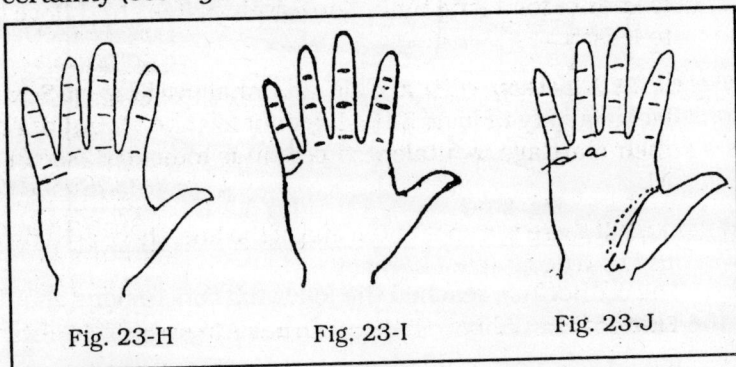

Fig. 23-H   Fig. 23-I   Fig. 23-J

• If there is a tassel or a trident at the end of the Line of Sexuality, love between the couple tends to diminish as time passes (see Fig. 23-K). If the line has two branches, love is diminished to some extent (see Fig. 23-L). If the branches go upwards, then the love between the partners is free from all defects.

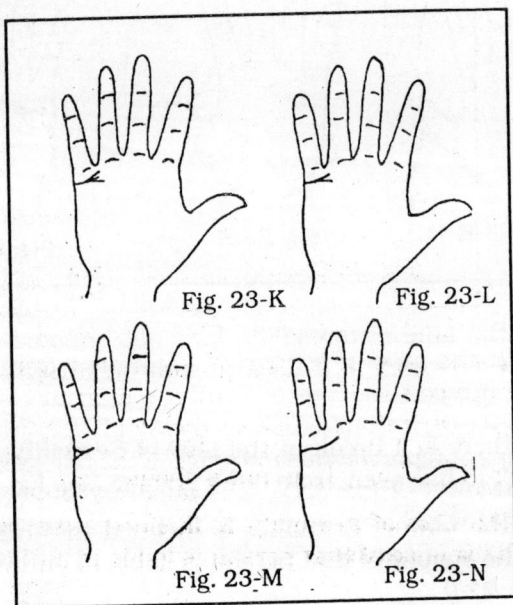

Fig. 23-K   Fig. 23-L

Fig. 23-M   Fig. 23-N

All the Secrets of Palmistry

• If there are two branches to this line in the beginning, before merging into one line, love between the couple tends to become intense as time passes *(see Fig. 23-M)*.

• If the Line of Sexuality is longer than usual, love tends to endure for a long time. Conversely, if it is short, love tends to lessen.

• A person with a wide and shallow Line of Sexuality lacks fidelity in love. If the line touches the Mount of Apollo, then marriage to a talented person is indicated *(see Fig. 23-N)*.

• If there is a spot at the end of the line, there are obstacles in the true course of love.

Indications of Marriage by Other Lines and Mounts

If the Mount of Venus is prominent, the person is likely to marry for physical pleasure.

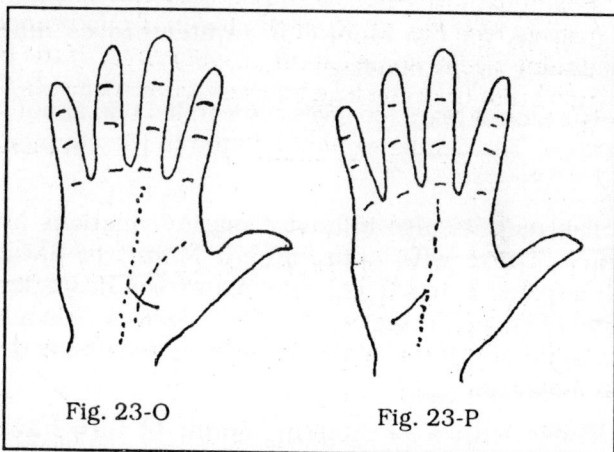

Fig. 23-O   Fig. 23-P

If the Line of Influence emanating from the Mount of Venus meets the Line of Saturn, a marriage is indicated *(see Fig. 23-O)*. If the line meets the Mount of Apollo, it means a happy and prosperous marriage. If the Line of Influence meets the Mount of Mercury, it is an unfortunate marriage. The age at which marriage is indicated can be calculated from the Line of Saturn.

If a person wants to marry for the sake of getting ahead in Life or for improving his career, it can be judged from the Line of Saturn. Lines of Influence emanating from the Mount of Moon before joining the Line of Saturn give an indication of marriage (see Fig. 23-P). The age at which marriage will take place can be calculated from the Line of Saturn. If the Line of Saturn remains deep and distinct after the Line of Influence touches it, the marriage proves fortunate. But if the Line of Saturn or Sun becomes defective, the marriage could turn into a misfortune. If the Line of Sun arises at that age, marriage brings good fortune and honour (see Fig. 23-Q). Both the palms should be studied before answering any question on the subject of marriage.

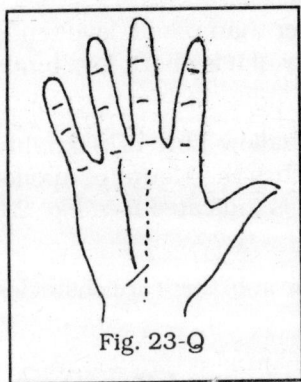

Fig. 23-Q

A cross on the Mount of Jupiter proves lucky and indicates a happy marriage.

The Line of Mars too gives some indication about marital relations. The details would be found in the chapter on the Line of Mars.

The mounts also influence marital relations and love affairs. Those with a prominent Mount of Saturn are disinterested in marriage. If such a person has a developed Mount of Venus, he seeks only physical pleasure in marriage. He is generally devoid of the sense of responsibility that goes with marriage.

Those with a prominent Mount of Sun have great expectations from their spouses. Tension can harm their marital relations easily.

Those with a prominent Mount of Mercury or Mars tend to marry early. Those who have a prominent Mount of Moon are disinterested in marriage. They marry only if their Lines of Sexuality are very strong, failing which, they are happy to remain single.

All the Secrets of Palmistry

XXIV

Line of Mars, Family Lines, Friend Lines and Enemy Lines

Many lines parallel to the Life Line are found on the Mount of Venus. The one nearest to the Life Line is called the Line of Mars (see Fig. 24-Aa). The lines next to it are called the Lines of Influence (see Fig. 24-Ab, Ac).

The Line of Mars rises from the Aggressive Mars and envelopes the Mount of Venus as it marches towards the wrist. Sometimes it stops after it has enveloped the Mount of Venus. This line is marked into segments to represent the age according to the rules applied to the Life Line.

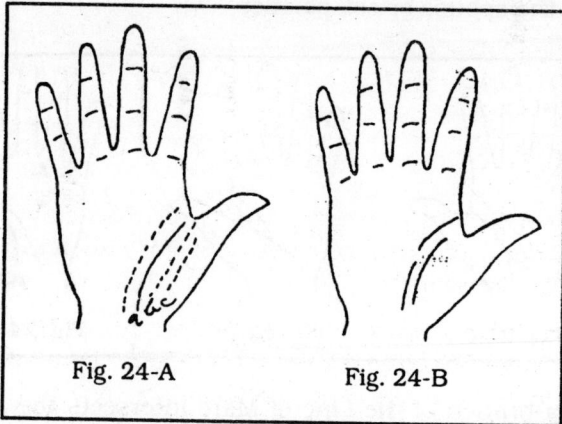

Fig. 24-A   Fig. 24-B

If this line is distinct and unbroken, the person is likely to remain healthy throughout his life. If the Life Line is defective and broken but the Line of Mars is excellent, it removes the faults of the Life Line (see Fig. 24-B). If the Line of Mars is short or is just not there on a palm, that person has little immunity against diseases.

Benham believes that the parallel line nearest to the Life Line is the Line of Parents; the line next to it is the Line of the Spouse and the other parallel lines, he says, indicate the number of friends and colleagues a person has.

The author's experience has led him to believe that the Line of Mars and the other lines running parallel to it indicate the number of colleagues and companions a person has (see Fig. 24-Aa, 24-Ab, 24-Ac). It can be said with confidence that if a person has lines on his Mount of Venus, and which are parallel to the Life Line, remains in good health with no major disease troubling him and continues to get cooperation from his parents, spouse, and near friends.

If the end of the Line of Mars divides into two branches to form a fork, the person is likely to lose his relationship with spouse (see Fig. 24-C). Some palmists believe that such a fork indicates separation in marriage or a break up. But to find a clear answer to this question, one also see the Line of Sexuality. If the line is defective, it means separation with either the spouse or sex partner.

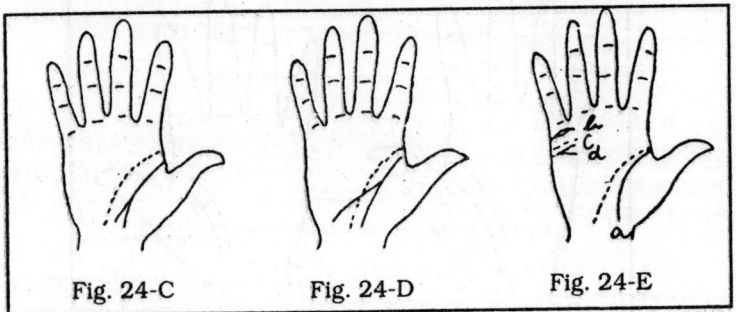

Fig. 24-C   Fig. 24-D   Fig. 24-E

If a branch of the Line of Mars intersects the Life Line and goes towards the Mount of Moon, it indicates a restless and disturbed disposition (see Fig. 24-D).

All the Secrets of Palmistry

If the Line of Mars is near the Life Line in the beginning, but the distance between them increases later on, it indicates that relations with a near relative would become distant (see Fig. 24-Ea). If the line is not broken or fragmented, a peaceful separation is indicated; otherwise, mutual recriminations would lead to separation. If along with this, there is a defect in the Line of Sexuality, it is a sure sign of lack of a strong bond with the spouse (see Fig. 24-Eb, Ec, Ed).

If the Line of Mars touches the Life Line, one's life might be in danger because of a near relative (see Fig. 24-F), but the Line of Sexuality should also be studied to be sure of this possibility. If that line is also defective, there might be a crisis or danger created by the spouse. The age at which this is possible can be found from the point of intersection of these lines on the Life Line.

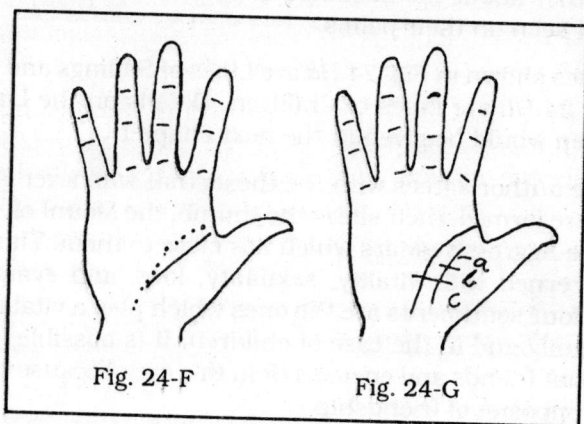

Fig. 24-F   Fig. 24-G

If there is a star on the Line of Mars, it presages some evil in the life of the nearest relation. If the Line of Sexuality is also defective, this line's influence affects the spouse; if it is not, then it applies to some other colleague/friend.

Horizontal lines on the Mount of Venus are called Worry Lines or lines which indicate obstacles (see Fig. 24-Ga). They represent problems or obstacles created by a person of the opposite sex. If they stop short of the Line of Mars, the worries or obstacles do not affect a person's life. But if they intersect the Line of Mars and stop short of the Life Line, their affect on life in minimal (see Fig. 24-Gb). If they intersect the Life

Line too *(see Fig. 24-Gc)*, the health of the person is likely to be affected. The effect depends on whether the Worry Lines are faint or deep. The time at which this is likely to happen can be calculated from the Life Line.

Lines moving from the Aggressive Mars towards the Life Line have a similar effect on the Line of Mars and the Life Line, while indicating that problems are caused by persons of the same sex. In other words, we can say that horizontal lines on the Mount of Venus and Aggressive Mars are Enemy Lines.

The author's experience and study indicate that these lines representing conjugal relationships or those of family relationships are formed only when a person cares for members of his family. In cases, however, where persons do not bother about the members of their families, such lines are not seen on their palms.

Lines shown in *Fig. 24-Ha* are Lines of Siblings and those in *Fig. 24-Hb* are Lines of Children. Details on the Lines of Children would be given in the next chapter.

The author agrees with the thesis that whenever Family Lines are formed, their site is the thumb, the Mount of Venus and the Aggressive Mars which lies close to them. This area is concerned with vitality, sexuality, love, and sympathy. These four sentiments are the ones which play a vital role in and family and in the case of children. It is possible to find out about friends and enemies from this area because enmity is the opposite of friendship.

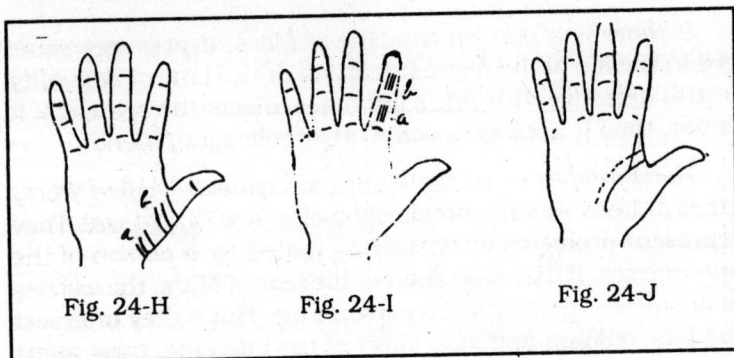

Fig. 24-H   Fig. 24-I   Fig. 24-J

All the Secrets of Palmistry

Lines of Friends and Enemies found at other sites in the palm are a subject of agreement among the palmists. Most of them believe that vertical lines on the phalanges of fingers and thumb indicate the number of friends a person has and those who are kindly disposed towards him (see Fig. 24-Ia). The lines which intersect these vertical lines indicate the number of enemies a person has (see Fig. 24-Ib). Sharp lines among them have a greater effect, whereas the faint ones have only a minimal effect.

We have spoken about parents and guardians when discussing the Line of Mars but now we come to signs which are found at other sites on the palm and which give a clue to a person's relations with his parents.

According to ancient Hindu palmistry, as mentioned in Samudrika Shastra, any line which emerges from the Mount of Jupiter meets the Line of Mars or touches it, then the person gets full love and affection from his/her parents (see Fig. 24-J). If any Line of Influence moves from the Mount of Jupiter to meet the Head Line, the person is likely to get his mother's love for a long time (see Fig. 24-K). Let it be clearly understood here that in some palms, the Head Line and the Life Line are one in the beginning. If, in such a case, the Line of Influence from the Mount of Jupiter meets the Head Line, it conveys that the person gets the affection of his parents in childhood and would continue to get it throughout his life.

If there is an island on the Line of Saturn rising from the wrist, the person is deprived of his parent's affection during childhood (see Fig. 24-L).

If the Heart Line starts with many branches, the person's parents live long (see Fig. 24-Ma) and if there is a sign of a fish on the Mount of Moon, the person inherits ancestral wealth (see Fig. 24-Mb).

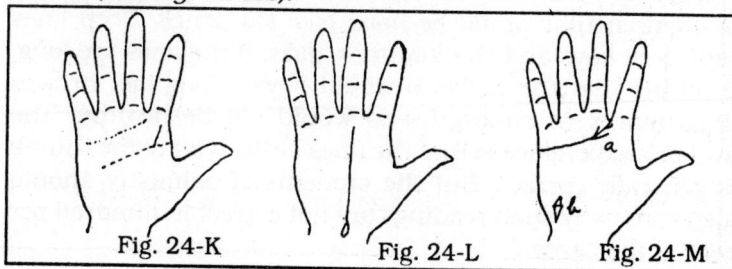

Fig. 24-K   Fig. 24-L   Fig. 24-M

XXV

Lines of Children

A question most often asked from palmists is how many children a person would have after marriage. Western palmists opine that the vertical lines on the Line of Sexuality or of Marriage represent the number of children (see Fig. 25-A). Well-defined lines indicate boys and the faint ones signify girls. But the author's experience is that answers based on this assumption is not correct.

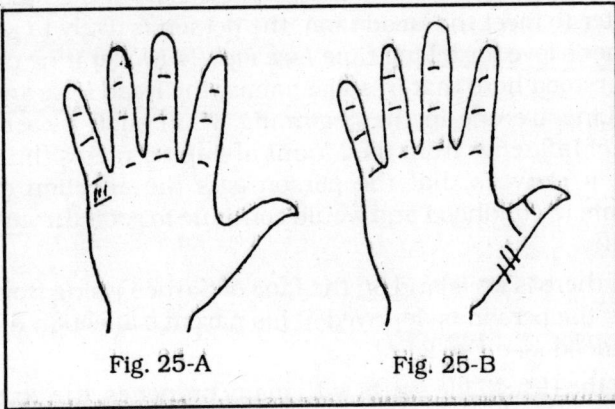

Fig. 25-A   Fig. 25-B

According to Samudrika Shastra, the vertical lines at the base of the thumb are the ones which represent the number of children that would be born (see Fig. 25-B). Deep lines represent boys and shallow ones, girls. If the lines are long, it means that the children would have a long life. Broken lines represent children who would not be healthy. The author's experience is that the lines at the base of the thumb is generally correct. But the students of palmistry should also know why such readings are not correct in hundred per cent of the cases.

What the Lines of Children indicate is the possibility that the sperm of the husband is strong enough to unite with the ova of the wife. But, sometimes, children are not born in spite of this. You can find the cause if the couple undergoes a medical examination. The husband might by carrying traces of a venereal infection and the wife might have traces of acidity or a defect in the uterus. That is why students are advised to study the palms of both the partners in a marriage.

The only thing that a palmist can say after examining the Lines of Children on the palm is whether the person has the capacity to procreate. If, in spite of that indication, there are no children, the answer can be found through a medical examination.

According to *Samudrika Shastra* there are islands in the basal region of the thumb, where it separates from the wrist. The number of children equals the number of these islands (*see Fig. 25-C*). The small islands represent girls and large ones, boys. The author has found this to be true in most cases.

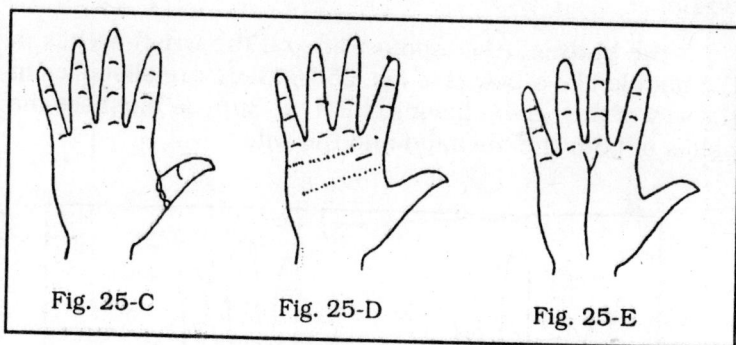

Fig. 25-C   Fig. 25-D   Fig. 25-E

If there is a horizontal line between the Head Line and the Heart Line which goes towards the Mount of Jupiter, a person is sure to have children (*see Fig. 25-D*).

If the Line of Saturn which starts from the wrist and ends in two branches, one going to the Mount of Saturn and the other to the Mount of Sun, there is every likelihood of children (*see Fig. 25-E*) being born.

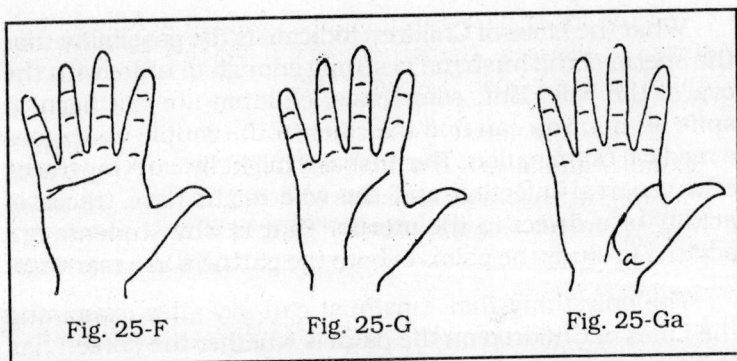

Fig. 25-F   Fig. 25-G   Fig. 25-Ga

Children are a certainty if the Heart Line ends in two branches, one going to the Mount of Mercury and the other to Defensive Mars (see Fig. 25-F).

If the Life Line is well-defined, and arises from the Mount of Jupiter (see Fig. 25-G) or if a branch of the line goes towards the Mount of Venus, enveloping it completely, then the person is likely to become father/mother of many children (see Fig. 25-Ga).

If the bracelet (the topmost line on the wrist) arches in the middle like a bow (see Fig. 25-H), there are obstacles in the way of the person having children. But you must see the palms of both the husband and the wife.

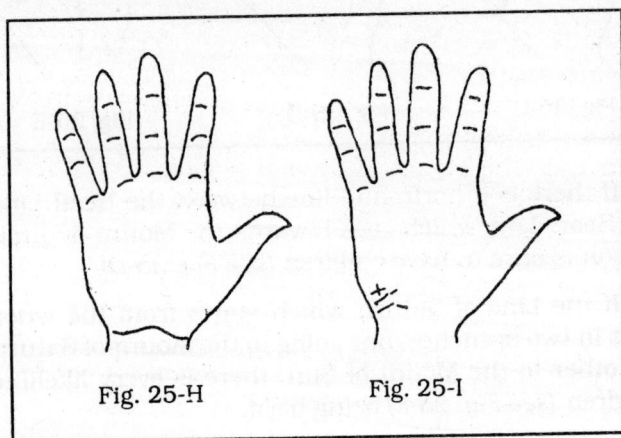

Fig. 25-H   Fig. 25-I

If the lower part of the Mount of Moon is full of broken lines, or crosses, then there are obstacles in the way of children being born (see Fig. 25-I).

One thing must be understood in this connection: sexuality and having children are two different things and a wife might be unable to produce children, because a child results when the sperm of the husband fertilises the ova of the wife. Sexuality, of course, depends on the presence of the hormone oestrogen in the female and androgen in the male, whereas infertility might be due to the failure of the sperm and the ova to meet.

Lines of Children might be found on the palms of eternal bachelors and those who have taken a vow of celibacy. Also women who have lost their husbands before they could consummate their marriage have Lines of Children. This shows that the Lines of Children only indicate the possibility of children. Failure of the sperm to fertilise the ovum renders the Lines of Children of little consequence. Practice of family planning methods produces similar results. That is why a palmist, while answering questions about children, should only indicate the possibility and say nothing more.

While answering questions about children, the palms of both the spouses should be examined and if either of them lacks the capacity to procreate, as indicated by the lines, the Mount of Venus and the Aggressive Mars should be studied. If the Mount of Venus is underdeveloped, the person should be advised to wear a diamond ring. If the Mount of Mars is underdeveloped, he should wear a coral ring and if the lower portion of the Mount of Moon is full of broken or fragmented lines, he should be advised to wear a pearl ring. In case the Mount of Jupiter is defective, a topaz ring is advisable.

XXVI

Travel Lines

An intense desire for change is the prime reason for travel. A person might go on a journey for business, employment or merely for pleasure.

Lines signifying the desire for change are found at the following sites:

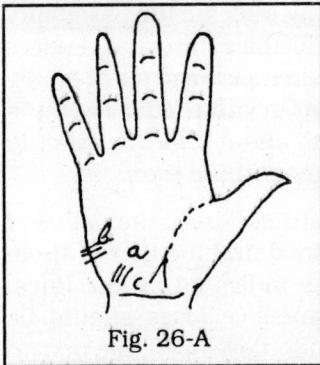

Fig. 26-A

• Vertical lines going from the wrist to the Mount of Moon (see Fig. 26-Aa).

• Horizontal lines on the percussion of the palm (see Fig. 26-Ab).

• Lines emanating from the Life Line and going towards the Mount of Moon (see Fig. 26-Ac).

One must study the quality of the hand while answering questions about possibilities of travel. If the hand is hard, the desire for travel is fulfilled, but if it is flabby, the desire for travel, though intense, is not fulfilled. If the first phalange of the thumb is long, there is possibility of travel, as is the case when the Mount of Moon and the Mount of Mercury are developed. If the whorls on the tips of the fingers are more in number than ordinarily found in most hands, travel lines are more effective.

According to ancient belief, the lines on the Mount of Moon presage sea voyages. There are two reasons for this belief:

All the Secrets of Palmistry

First, according to ancient sages and seers, the moon is connected to water and secondly, the only way to go abroad was though a sea voyage. Now short journeys are undertaken by train and longer by air. That is why the interpretation of these lines has changed.

In modern-day palmistry, deep and long lines indicate long voyages or journeys and short lines signify journeys within the country. Let it be understood that sudden journeys or those undertaken in emergencies are not indicated on the palm.

Vertical lines going from the wrist to the Mount of Moon point towards the possibility of important voyages (see Fig. 26-B). These lines also point to the possibility of the person rising in stature because of such journeys.

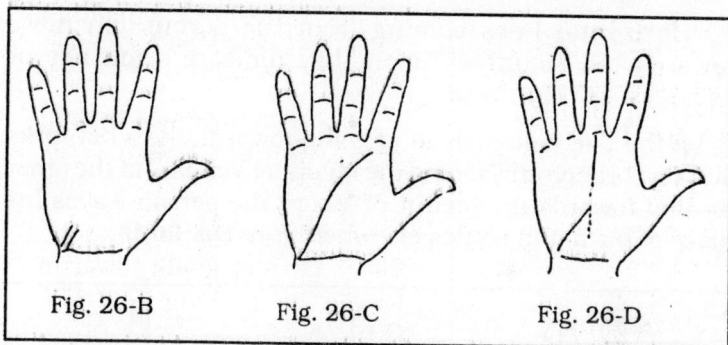

Fig. 26-B   Fig. 26-C   Fig. 26-D

If a line emanating from the wrist and going via the Mount of Moon reaches the Mount of Jupiter, the voyage is a lucky one (see Fig. 26-C). But this line has to be differentiated from the Line of Saturn. If the line emanating from the wrist goes from the Mount of Moon and meets the Line of Saturn, it could be a sign of travel (see Fig. 26-D), but if the Line of Saturn becomes defective after that, it could bring ill luck. The time at which such a journey would be undertaken can be calculated from the point at which the line meets the Line of Saturn.

If the line remains the same or improves, then travel proves lucky.

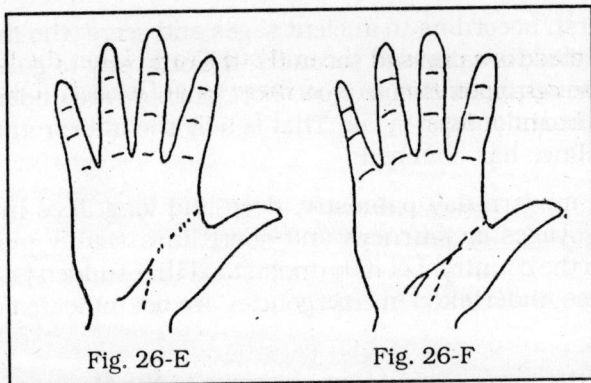

Fig. 26-E   Fig. 26-F

If the Line of Travel emanates from the Life Line and goes towards the Mount of Moon, it indicates travel (see Fig. 26-E). If the Travel Line divides into two branches, there will be trouble during the voyage (see Fig. 26-F).

Horizontal lines coming from the percussion move towards the Mount of Moon they indicate a journey or journeys (see Fig. 26-G).

If the Life Line instead of going towards the wrist forks out, one branch enveloping the Mount of Venus and the other moving towards the Mount of Moon, the person leaves his place of birth and settles elsewhere (see Fig. 26-H).

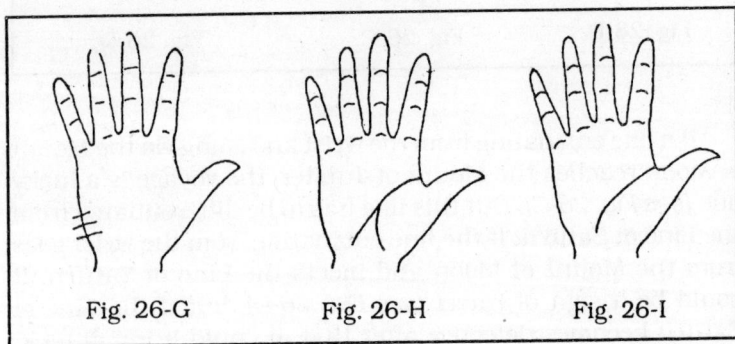

Fig. 26-G   Fig. 26-H   Fig. 26-I

If the Life Line instead of enveloping the Mount of Venus goes towards the Mount of Moon, the life of a person is spent in travel and he does not return to his country of birth (see Fig. 26-I).

All the Secrets of Palmistry

If there is a cross at the end of a Travel Line, the journey will be disappointing and if there is an island, it leads to some harm or loss.

XXVII

Rascette or Bracelet

Some horizontal lines are found on the wrist and these resemble a bracelet. They are called Bracelets or Rascettes (*see Fig. 27-A*). The first bracelet from the palm facing the arms is called the First Bracelet or Rascette and the others are second, third and so on.

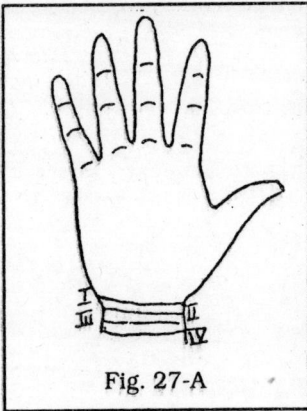

Fig. 27-A

Great importance is given to bracelets according to Hindu palmistry. Each bracelet is supposed to represent an age of 30 years. If a person has four, clear and well-defined bracelets, he should live up to 120 years of age. If the lines are incomplete or indistinct, it indicates a short age and unhealthy life.

St. Germain believes that each bracelet represents an age of 25 to 27 years and that if a person has four bracelets, he should live to be a 100-years old.

According to modern palmistry, if there is a first well-defined bracelet, it indicates excellent health. If it is indistinct, it presages loss of vital energy. The first bracelet, if it has chains on it, indicates a life full of struggle.

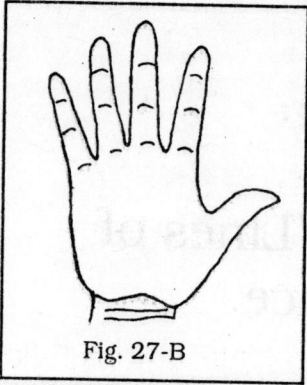

Fig. 27-B

If the first bracelet arches upwards like a bow *(see Fig. 27-B)*, then there are obstructions in the birth of children. If the lower part of the Mount of Moon is also defective, this tendency gets accentuated.

A star or cross on the first bracelet indicates a life of difficulty and struggle.

Modern palmists do not give much importance to the second, the third and the fourth bracelets.

XXVIII

Minor Lines/Lines of Influence

This category includes lines which are found on the palms of very few persons. These are:

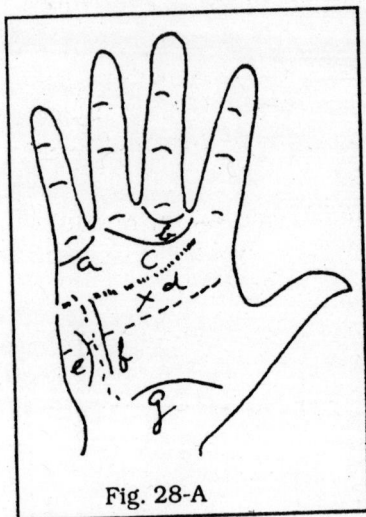

Fig. 28-A

- Ring of Solomon (see Fig. 28-Aa).
- Ring of Saturn (see Fig. 28-Ab).
- Girdle of Venus (see Fig. 28-Ac).
- Mystic Cross (see Fig. 28-Ad).
- Line of Intuition (see Fig. 28-Ae).
- Via Lasciva (see Fig. 28-Afd).
- Influence Lines/Chance Lines.

Ring of Solomon

This is like a bow which lies between the Mount of Jupiter and the index finger (see Fig. 28-B). It indicates wisdom and stops a person from taking to evil ways. Persons with the Ring of Solomon are interested in research and in

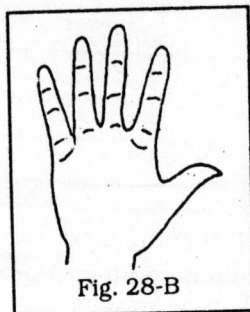

Fig. 28-B

192

All the Secrets of Palmistry

occult sciences. If the Head Line of such a person is good, the qualities of the Ring of Solomon increase.

If there is also the Line of Intuition, a person has occult powers like persons who have attained *siddhi* (sages with supernatural powers).

The Ring of Solomon is not always like a perfect bow; generally two lines coming from two different directions manage to form an incomplete bow. The effect of such an incomplete ring is, naturally, less than that of a full ring.

Ring of Saturn

This is like a bow between the middle finger and the Mount of Saturn. It may be found complete in some palms and incomplete in others (*see Fig. 28-C*).

Persons with a complete Ring of Saturn are likely to have an unstable character. They cannot give their complete attention to anything; instead, they change their profession from time to time.

The presence of a cross or other defects on the Mount of Moon alongwith the Ring of Saturn is liable to make a person ill tempered. He might even try to commit suicide.

An incomplete Ring of Saturn is less inauspicious than a complete one (*see Fig. 28-D*).

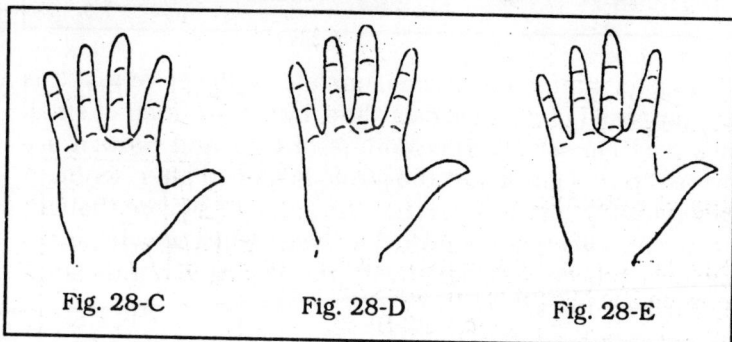

Fig. 28-C   Fig. 28-D   Fig. 28-E

If the Ring of Saturn is not like a bow, but is formed by two lines coming from opposite directions and intersecting each other (*see Fig. 28-E*), it has the same effect as that of a cross on the Mount of Saturn. In other words, it signifies ill luck. The time of life when ill luck would strike can be calculated according to the rule which applies to calculation of age from the Line of Saturn.

Girdle of Venus

This girdle starts in the shape of a bow from the middle of the little and the ring finger and goes to a point in the middle of the second and first finger (see Fig. 28-F). It envelopes the Mounts of Sun and Saturn.

It is found in a perfect bow shape in very rare hands. Normally two lines coming from different directions move towards each other and stop before they can complete the half circle. Such a girdle is called a Broken Girdle of Venus (see Fig. 28-G).

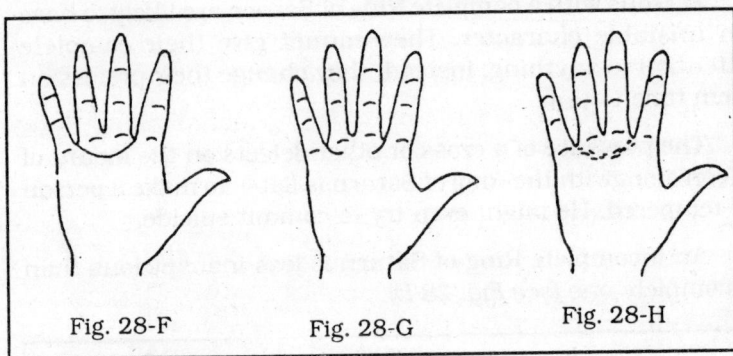

Fig. 28-F   Fig. 28-G   Fig. 28-H

In some hands there is a complete Girdle of Venus. It is not composed of a single clear line, but of a bunch of small lines (see Fig. 28-H). The Mounts of Sun and Saturn are covered in this girdle but the girdle is named after Venus. A reason for this probably is that the palmists of yore thought that it was somehow connected with sexuality, which in turn has always been associated with the Mount of Venus since the earliest times.

The author, considers it as a subsidiary of the Heart Line.

If the Girdle of Venus is well-defined and complete, it is indicative of the sensitivity in a person. If a palm is devoid of the Heart Line, the Girdle of Venus can be taken to act as its substitute.

The girdle can be associated with sexuality only if the Line of Mars is deep and red, the Aggressive Mars and the Mount of Venus are developed and the little finger is longer than usual. If these signs are not present, this girdle can only be interpreted to indicate the sensitivity of the nervous system; in other words, the susceptibility to psychological tensions.

This line is not found in square and hard or rough hands. The girdle is more in evidence in long, narrow and psychic palms. If it is found in a hard and square hand, it does not have the same effect as it has in others. If it is found in soft and flabby hands, it might lead to hysteria and even insanity.

A broken Girdle of Venus does not have much effect. A girdle formed with small lines indicates excessive mental activity. It tends to create a sense of unease, impatience and nervousness.

If the Girdle of Venus is found in hands which have developed Mounts of Saturn and Moon, it tends to create indecisiveness in the person whose thinking, therefore, becomes negative.

If the Line of Sexuality touches the Girdle of Venus, the person expects too much from his/her spouse. These expectations tend to remain unfulfilled, leading to increase in his dissatisfaction and depression.

A good, straight Head Line tends to rectify the negative effect of the Girdle of Venus. If the Head Line is broken or goes towards the Mount of Moon, the possibility of the person suffering from mental disorders like hysteria and epilepsy is increased.

A long thumb with a long first phalange tends to neutralise the negative effect of the Girdle of Venus. If the second phalange of the thumb is large, indecisiveness tends to increase in a person.

Mystic Cross

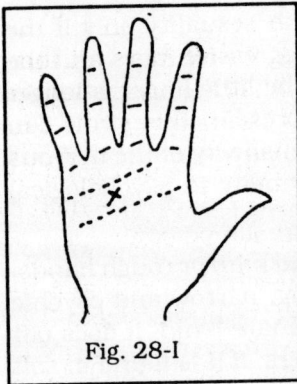

Fig. 28-I

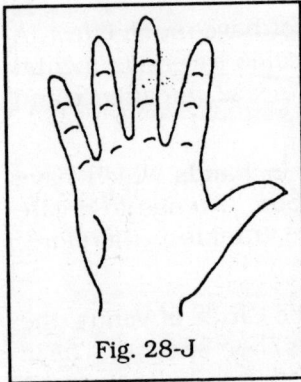

Fig. 28-J

A cross lying in the middle of the Head Line and the Heart Line is called the Mystic Cross. It may resemble the sign of addition or multiplication *(see Fig. 28-I)*.

The Mystic Cross is the one formed by the Lines of Influence. If it is formed by the intersection of the main or secondary lines, it is a simple cross and does not fall in the category of a Mystic Cross.

According to ancient palmists, a person with a Mystic Cross on his palm has the ability to go into the finer points of occult. If such a cross is accompanied by the Line of Intuition, the person can look into the past, present and the future *(see* the Line of Intuition *in Fig. 28-J)*.

The author believes that the Mystic Cross has its peculiar significance only if it is accompanied by the Line of Intuition. But this cross is not a negative factor. If there are many crosses at the site of this cross, it indicates restlessness of the spirit.

Line of Intuition

Knowledge of the world comes to us from the sense organs, traditionally five in number. They are eyes, ears, nose, skin and the tongue. The sixth sense organ is the mind.

The mind is the most developed among the organs of sense. A developed mind has limitless capabilities. It can

All the Secrets of Palmistry

see without the eye, hear without the ear, smell without the nose, touch without the skin, taste without using the tongue, fly thousands of miles without wings and see into the past, the present and the future.

There is no scientific explanation for all this, but there are countless examples where the truth of the mind attaining the highest from of development has been proved.

The mental capacities of a person are evident from his palm. It is the Line of Intuition (see Fig. 28-J) which is indicative of the mental development of a person.

This line is found on the mount which represents the quality of imagination, a peculiarity of the human mind. This line is seen in the palms of persons with a very strong mind. That is why the author has named the Line of Intuition as the Line of Moon.

The Mount of Moon lies on the path of the Line of Mercury, but that line is not semi-circular or shaped like a bow. This is the difference between the Line of Mercury and the Line of Intuition.

This line is in evidence generally on a philosopher's or a psychic hand. If it is well-defined on a palm, then that person is able to know what is in the mind of another person. If this line is broken, the faculty of intuition is reduced.

If there is an island on the Line of Intuition, the person is liable to be a sleepwalker. If horizontal lines intersect this line, there are obstacles in the way of achievements. The horizontal lines take on the qualities of the mount from which they arise. If there is a Line of Intuition on a palm and the Head Line is inclined towards the Mount of Moon, the power of intuition tends to increase (see Fig. 28-K). If with this combination a Mystic Cross is present on that palm, then the mental capacity of such a person is limitless.

Via Lasciva

Palmists do not agree on the significance of this line. St. Germain and Benham are of the view that Via Lasciva is a

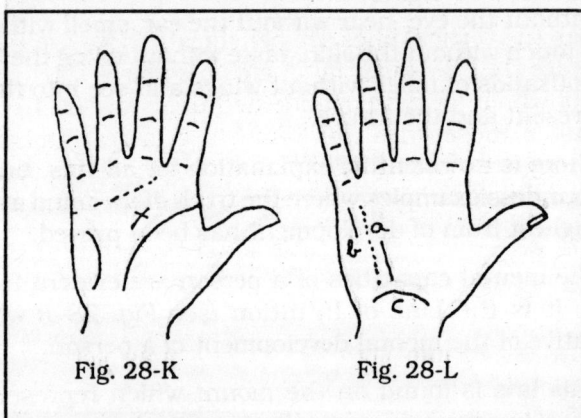

Fig. 28-K   Fig. 28-L

short line running parallel to the Line of Mercury on the Mount of Moon *(see Fig. 28-La or Lb)*. This line tends to strengthen the Line of Mercury and its force lies in the extra sexuality in a person.

Some palmists are of the view that this line is a sort of bridge between the Mount of Venus and the Mount of Moon. It is generally in the shape of a bow *(see Fig. 28-Lc)*.

If the Via Lasciva is found on a soft and thin hand, then the person has a strong sexuality which does not take a physical form. Such a person is more liable to be addicted to liquor and other habit-forming drugs.

If such a person has a weak Head Line and a short thumb, with a long first phalange, he is likely to lose all sense of discrimination when it comes to satisfying his sexuality.

If Via Lasciva intersects the Life Line after which the latter becomes weak, a person is likely to suffer from health problems because of his sexuality. Such an intersection of lines is found on very few hands.

Chance Lines

You would see many vertical, horizontal and oblique lines on the palm. No name has been given to them. They are called Chance Lines and indicate intense mental activity. They take on the qualities of the mount on which they are found. Horizontal lines indicate harm caused by that mount, whereas the vertical lines are beneficial. These are the lines which are the raw material of cross, square, star, etc., the effect of which we have commented upon in the chapter on mounts. If these lines are found in a large number on a palm, they are indicative of the multi-dimensional activity of the mind. Such a mind might be called a multi-channel mind.

Important Guidelines in Practice of Palmistry

XXIX

How to Study the Hand

The first question is from which point does one begin to read the lines on the hand. It is better to make a check-list on a piece of paper so that you do not miss any of the signs. The check list should be in the order of the signs to be studied. The author has a check-list for hand-reading which requires more time to be given to it. A sample check-list is given on the next page.

The author believes that the palmist should study the hand to find the favourable aspects. It is the favourable lines and signs which should be interpreted first of all for the benefit of the client.

Many palms do not have good signs which could be the starting point for you to give a reading. But if you look closely, you will find some positive sign or the other. You should stress on good signs before you start reading the hand. It will give the client a cause for hope.

After you have dealt with the good signs, come to the bad ones. But be careful in the choice of words while dealing with bad aspects of the palm. A bitter pill, you should remember, should always be sugar-coated. If there are good signs in one hand and bad ones in the other, then explain in detail only the positive aspects. If both the hands carry bad signs, tell the client so but also tell him the remedies to convert the bad into good. It should be remembered that the lines of the palm continue to change, though the fingerprints do not. This we had stated in an earlier chapter too. The remedies to offset the bad aspects of a hand would be dealt with in the next chapter.

If the answer to any of the client's question is likely to cause disappointment, sugar-coat your answer. It is the duty of a palmist to give a ray of hope to a despondent client.

Remedies to offset the evil effects of negative signs are mentioned in the next chapter.

Check-list

Date   Name   Age or *Date of Birth*
Specific Question   *Active Hand:*
                                                   Right/Left

Active Hand	Inactive Hand
1. Category/shape/colour of hand	
2. Colour/quality of lines	
3. Finger/inclination/speciality/setting	
4. Thumb/inclination/shape/setting	
5. Which phalange of thumb is long?	
6. Developed mounts	
7. Underdeveloped mounts	
8. Fingerprints	
9. Life Line, origin direction end	
10. Head Line, origin direction end	
11. Heart Line, origin direction end	
12. Saturn Line, origin direction end	
13. Sun Line, origin direction end	
14. Line of Mercury, origin direction end	
15. Lines of Sexuality	
16. Line of Mars	
17. Lines of Children	
18. Travel Lines	
19. Girdle of Venus	
20. Ring of Solomon	
21. Ring of Saturn	
22. Line of Intuition	
23. Via Lasciva	
24. Bracelets	
25. Remedies to counter the defects of various lines/mounts	
26. Good signs on hand	
27. Bad signs on hand	

Note down the peculiarities, signs on the palms in code/ brief. You could have a code which uses a tick mark for a normal mount, plus sign for a developed mount and sign of deduction for an underdeveloped mount. You can have your own code according to your convenience.

XXX

Remedies for Defective Lines and Mounts

It is vital for readers to know about the remedies to correct the defects of the mounts or lines on the palm, because unless palmists can give relief to their clients, it is no good reading their palms.

Digital Postures

We said in the beginning that according to physiology, a larger part of the brain is concerned with the movement of the fingers than the other organs of the body.

If you cast your eye on the yogic postures which the practitioners of this noble art adopt, you would notice that while the sages of old went into meditation, they positioned their fingers in certain ways. This is clear when seen from the ancient statues of the Jain *Tirathankaras* and Lord Buddha.

From a study of modern physiology and yoga, the author has reached the conclusion that the purpose of the peculiar positioning of the fingers by the sages of old was to transfer the surplus energy of certain centres of the brain to other areas, in order to bring a balanced state of mind and body.

Having studied the subject, i.e. the role which fingers or digital postures play, and also having sought the guidance of sages and wise men adept in this art, the author has gained certain knowledge which he would like to pass on to his readers. As a palmist he has used this knowledge to remove the evil effects of the defective mounts and lines of the palm and has found that it has helped many persons. Read further to find the remedies.

All the Secrets of Palmistry

Digital Postures to Strengthen the Heart

This is a position or posture in which the tips of the first three fingers touch the tip of the thumb (see Fig. 30-A). If the Heart Line is defective or the Mount of Sun is overdeveloped or there is an underdeveloped Mount of Moon, this posture helps. Those suffering from hypertension or a heart ailment or have suffered a heart attack, should try this posture every day. They should keep the fingers in this position for 15 minutes in the morning and for an equal time in the evening. But if your client is taking medicines on the advice of the physician for these ailments, he should not be asked to discontinue the course of treatment, while continuing with this exercise.

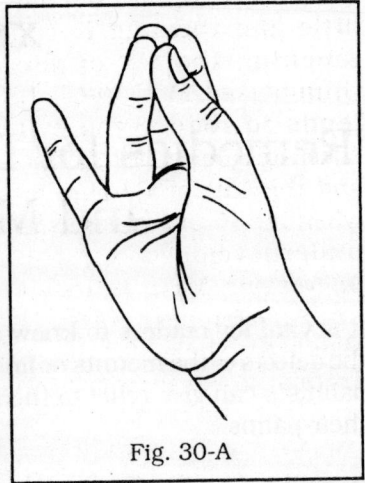

Fig. 30-A

Digital Posture to Strengthen the Brain

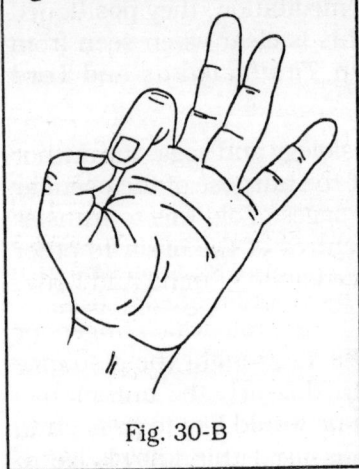

Fig. 30-B

The posture of the fingers consists in the tips of the first finger and the tip of the thumb meeting each other (see Fig. 30-B). In yoga, it is called the *chinmudra*. If the Head Line is defective and the Mount of Jupiter is either overdeveloped or underdeveloped, it helps to remove the defects. Those placed in such a situation should practice this posture for 15 minutes in the morning and for an equal time in the evening.

Posture to Increase the Vital Force

It consists of tips of both the little and the ring finger touching the tip of the thumb *(see Fig. 30-C)*. It tends to reduce the evil effects of a defective Life Line and the Line of Mercury or when the Mount of Venus is underdeveloped or the Aggressive Mars is in an underdeveloped state. It should also be practiced for 15 minutes in the morning and 15 in the evening.

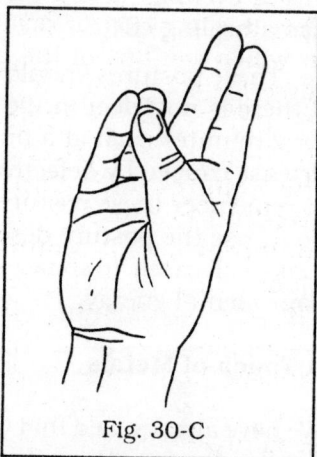

Fig. 30-C

Postures to Remove the Defects of Saturn

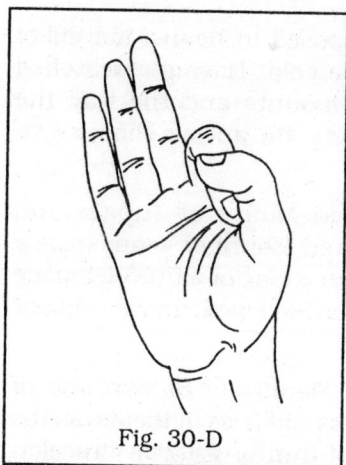

Fig. 30-D

Bend the index finger so that its tip touches the Mount of Venus and keep the other fingers away *(see Fig. 30-D)*. This posture helps to correct the defects of the mount and the Line of Saturn. It should also be practiced for 15 minutes in the morning and 15 min. in the evening. Extra time should be given to this exercise in case a person with a defective Mount of Saturn suffers from diseases like paralysis, gout and pain in the joints, which are caused by vitiation of *vayu* (gas).

Digital Posture to Remove Defects of Mercury

This posture entails in touching the combined first and middle fingers of the right hand with the tip of the index finger of the left. If the mount and the Line of Mercury are both defective, practise this posture with both the hands for a quarter of an hour in the morning and for the same time in the evening. If you suffer from flatulence, this posture has a healing effect.

These postures should be repeated with both the hands. If there is no defect in the lines, practising all the postures for 2 minutes each at a time wards off the possibility of any disease caused by defective mounts and lines. It is not easy to remember these postures all the time. If you forget how to do it, use the posture described in *Fig. 30-B* which helps in almost all cases, to some extent, because it tends to augment your mental energy.

A Touch of Metals

We have already said that the Aggressive Mars is a hot planet. Jupiter, Sun and Venus have a moderately hot effect. Mercury is less hot, while Saturn and Moon are cold and Defensive Mars is less cold.

As for metals, copper is supposed to have a hot effect whereas iron is considered to be cold. Having researched into the effects of the various mounts and the way the different metals set off these effects, the author shares with you his conclusions.

Persons with underdeveloped Mount of Jupiter and Mount of Sun, Aggressive Mars and Mount of Venus have a weak heart and are advised to wear a ring or a bracelet made of copper. If these mounts are overdeveloped, an iron ring or iron bracelet is the answer.

Those with underdeveloped Mounts of Saturn and of Moon and Defensive Mars have less coolness in their systems and should wear a ring made of iron or an iron bracelet. Conversely, if these mounts are overdeveloped, a copper ring or a copper bracelet is ideal to wear.

The iron ring should be worn on the middle finger of the active hand or an iron bracelet on the wrist of such a hand. The copper ring should be worn on the ring finger of the active hand or a copper bracelet on the active wrist. Wearing these rings or bracelets tends to reduce the evil effects of the mounts.

All the Secrets of Palmistry

If both the hot and cold mounts are underdeveloped, wear both iron and copper rings or bracelets. If mounts of both the categories are well developed, one need not wear any such ring or bracelet. For defects in the lines of the hand, exercising in different digital postures as indicated earlier provides the answer.

Worship and Rituals

Some people tend to suffer from the fear that somebody is performing some religious ritual to harm them. They should be advised to undertake worship of their favourite deities to invoke their blessings through recitation of prayers and *mantras*. Such practices boost their morale and also ward off the evil, but always advise your client not to insist on performing a ritual intended to harm another person. Ill will towards another tends to cloud one's mind, pushing the person towards ill luck instead of good fortune.

Removal of Tension Through *Swara-Yoga*

A person who has a mesh of lines on his palm and horizontal stripes on his nails is generally a victim of tension and depression. He also suffers from insomnia because he is always worried as how to achieve his ambitions. He should be advised to strengthen his *chandra swara*. How to operate the *swaras*, in other words, how to control your breathing is described in the following paragraphs so that you can help your client to overcome his tension and depression.

It is easy to stop breathing from one nostril and to start from the other.

But, before you recommend exercises in breath control, you must try it out yourself. This is how you can recognise which of the nostrils is active at any particular time.

Close your mouth and press your right nostril with your finger, keeping the left one open. Exhale deeply. Then close your left nostril and breathe through the right one. Inhale deeply and then release your breath. After you have repeated this twice or thrice, you would know which one of your nostrils is active, i.e., through which hostril you are able to breathe easily.

If you can breathe easily from the right nostril, it means that the *surya swara* is stronger. If you can breathe easily from the left hostril it means that your *chandra swara* is stronger. If your breath comes with equal ease from both the nostrils, it is the *sushumna swara* which is predominant.

Each of the three *swaras* change after some time. When a person is bothered by tension, anger, depression or insomnia, it is the *surya swara* which is predominant. If you could change over to *chandra swara*, in other words, change over to breathing from your left nostril, tension gets reduced and sleep comes easily.

The *surya swara* helps in digestion, in situations of conflict, competition or sexual union.

If the *sushumna swara* continues for more than an hour, it is harmful. One must pray to one's favourite deity and seek his/her blessings to ward off the evil.

How to Change the *Swaras*?

If the *surya* is in operation and you want to switch over to the *chandra swara*, change your position in bed and lie on your right so that the right nostril touches the pillow and the left one is open to the ceiling. After about five minutes, you will find that the left nostril starts working. If it does not happen in the first five to seven minutes, continue with the posture and lie down for a longer period.

Conversely, if you want the *surya swara* to be active, lie on your left, keeping the right nostril up and the left one towards the pillow.

There are other methods too to change to *swaras*, about which more details are given in the author's book entitled *Dhyan Yoga*.

Other Methods

Just as looking at yourself daily in the mirror helps you to improve your looks, similarly looking at your hands first thing in the morning helps to improve your luck. An ancient *sloka* says:

Kragre vasate Lakshmi, karmadhyey Saraswati,
karprishthe tu Govinda, prabhate kar darshanam.

Meaning of Sloka

(Goddess Lakshmi – the goddess of wealth – resides in the upper part of the hand, that is, the fingers; Goddess Saraswati – the goddess of learning – resides in the middle of the palm. The back of the hand is the abode of Govinda, who is God and it is recommended that you must see your hands first thing in the morning).

While looking at your hands, you must concentrate on your favourite deity and seek his/her blessings. This gives a boost to your morale and the negative aspects of the hand get diluted.

Fasting for Good Luck

A friend of the author generally advises his clients to fast once a week or desist from eating a favourite food or dish. Some palmists/astrologers advise their clients to feed the birds every day. If a person has faith and fasts once a week or feeds the birds, it boosts his morale as it has a beneficial effect on his luck. But, without faith, no positive results can be expected from these practices. Digital postures and wearing metal rings and bracelets, however, have a decided effect, whether you have faith in the practice or not.

We have said in the beginning of this work that the lines of the palm continue to change, to become either positive or negative. The remedies mentioned in this chapter bring on positive changes and the lines too change positively. Let us recapitulate the remedies:

- Digital postures.

- Wearing metal rings or bracelets.

- Practising *swara yoga.*

- Looking at the hands in the morning while meditating on your favourite deity.

- Fasting, etc.

You can suggest any one or more of the remedies to your clients depending on their beliefs and faith.

XXXI

Practical Palmistry

So far we have dealt with the theoretical aspects of palmistry. We must now come to the practical aspect.

You will find the handprints of two persons in this chapter (see Figs. 31-AB and Fig. 31-CD). Let us now learn how to read these palms.

Handprint in Fig. 31-AB

These handprints belongs to a housewife of 54 yrs. who had asked a question pertaining to her health.

A multiplicity of lines on the palm might lead to the impression that she is given to worrying. In other words, she thinks too much. Where there are crosses because of the multiplicity of lines, you would find squares too and that is why it can be said that these lines do not affect her luck. The prominence of mounts do not appear in a handprint and that is why the author noted the chief features of her palms at the time of taking the handprint. They are:

The Aggressive and Defensive Mars are underdeveloped. The Mount of Jupiter is overdeveloped and the skin of the palms is flexible.

The reason that the Aggressive Mars is underdeveloped points to the fact that she is not assertive and likes to avoid trouble if she can. The Defensive Mars too is underdeveloped, indicating her becoming despondent in times of trouble. The prominence of the Mount of Jupiter attests to her preference for honour as compared to material goods. All the other mounts are normally developed which are indicative of good fortune.

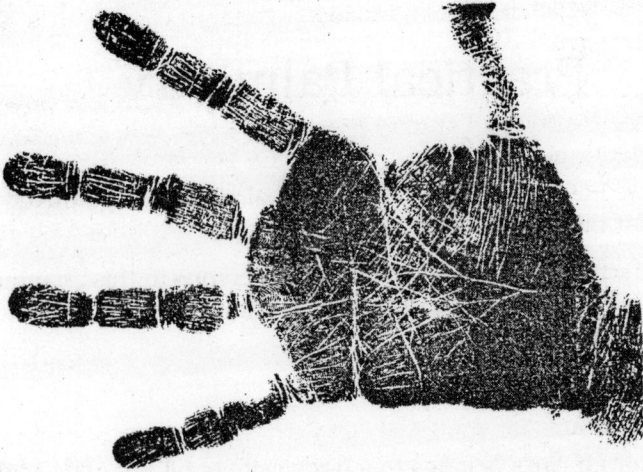

Fig. 31B (Left)

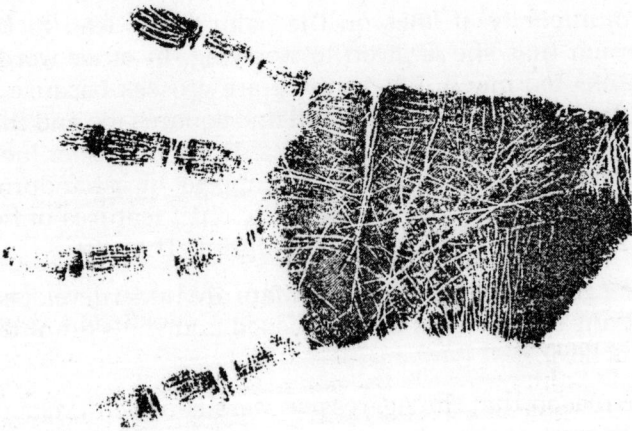

Fig. 31A (Right)

All the Secrets of Palmistry

While studying the other signs, the author found that the index and the middle fingers incline towards the ring finger, while the ring finger and the little finger inclined towards the middle finger signifying absence of a point towards which her thoughts are turned. In other words, she is indecisive.

The skin of her palms is flexible and when the fingers and the thumb are spread like a Japanese fan, the fingers and the thumb point outwards which signify that she is not fixed in her ideas and has the quality of adjusting herself to the circumstances. There are loops in abundance on her fingertips which again reveal her accommodative nature. The second phalange of the thumb is large which means that her thought processes are very strong. The first phalange of the thumb is small, testifying to her inability to put her thoughts into action.

These are the details of the various signs on her palms; now it is for the readers to decide what should be told to her, after, or course, they have studied all the signs.

Now let us come to the lines on the right palm. The Line of Saturn originates from the middle of the Life Line and is well defined. There are small breaks in the line but in spite of them, the line is clear and travels a long distance, indicating good fortune but with some obstacles.

The Head Line and the Life Line are one till the age of 20 and this part is composed of chains. It means that till the age of 20, the woman suffered from a sense of inferiority and her health had been indifferent. The rest of the Head Line in both the palms is good. In the left palm the subsidiary or secondary line runs parallel to the Head Line, which in the right palm goes up to the percussion and is forked at the end. This indicates wisdom and the woman will continue to possess this quality till the end.

The Life Line is intersected by Lines of Worry coming from Aggressive Mars, representing obstacles created by the members of the family. These tend to adversely affect her health. But despite these obstacles, the Life Line continues to be deep and clear, indicating that the obstacles are being removed.

The reason for this is a good Line of Mars and its parallel line. Most Lines of Worry stop at the Line of Mars indicating that it is her husband who removes the obstacles which come in her way. The line running parallel to the Line of Mars points towards another member of the family who is helpful. That member could be one of her parents or a sibling. The lines which produce the obstacles intersect the Life Line till the age of 30 and later they affect only the Line of Mars. It can be interpreted to mean that after the age of 30, there are no obstacles in her life.

Let us now come to the Line of Saturn. In the right palm this line originates from the Life Line. It is broken in the middle at four points but in spite of that, it continues to be deep. The Line of Saturn crosses the Heart Line and is positive till the age of 60. This is the palm of a housewife whose only source of income is the earnings of her husband. The Line of Saturn in her palm points to the income of her husband and also the fact that she is thrifty.

There are two Lines of Saturn in the left palm — one originating from the Life Line and the other from the Mount of Moon. The line coming from the Mount of Moon reveals that the income comes from outside the family. The other Line of Saturn originates from the Life Line. In both the palms the point of separation of the Line of Saturn from the Life Line shows 30 years. It means that for the first 30 years of her life the woman was under the influence of a joint family after which her husband had two sources of income — one is business which he inherited from his family and the other is which he built up with his own sagacity. If we study closely the Line of Saturn in both the palms, we can see that till the age of 60 her husband's income would be considerable. The various breaks in the line point to the fact that most of the time her husband's income has been limited and he had to face economic stringency, though infrequently.

After the age of 60, there are three vertical lines on the Mount of Saturn. Similar lines can be seen on the Mount of Sun. These lines are intersected by a broken Girdle of Venus which also intersects the vertical lines on the Mount of Sun, indicating that in the last part of her life she is likely to develop the habit to worry. But, because of the Mount of

Sun, she is likely to earn fame. This Line of Fame is intersected at the age of 80 but should not be a matter of concern because after the age of 80, the Life Line becomes indistinct. We can interpret this to mean that at the end of her life, there would be new sources of income. She would no longer suffer any problems because she now has old sources of income.

The vertical lines on the Mount of Mercury show that she is wise in money matters and tries new experiments at saving expenses in household matters. She is interested in gardening and cooking, which are a part of good housekeeping.

Let us now turn to the main question which bothers her, namely, her health. The answer to this can be found in three lines — the Line of Mercury, the Head Line, the Heart Line and the Lines of Worry on Aggressive Mars.

The Heart Line originates from the Mount of Jupiter indicating a desire to experience new forms of love and affection. There is a light Ring of Solomon which prevents her from evil ways, but the islands on the Heart Line are indicative of emotional shocks she is liable to get. The fact that the Mount of Jupiter is overdeveloped and the intersection by Lines of Worry on the Aggressive Mars with the Life Line bear testimony to her desire for honour which is not fulfilled, and hence her troubles. She gave love and affection to those around her, but never did they reciprocate her love. On the other hand, they only created obstacles in her path.

The Line of Mercury originates from the Life Line in the right palm at the age of 50, but in the left palm this line originates from the Life Line at 60 years. In the left palm one branch of the Line of Mercury goes towards the Defensive Mars which has two further sections — one going to Mount of Mercury and the other running parallel to the Line of Saturn. This is a bad sign for her health. Look at the Mount of Moon in both the palms and you will notice that the middle of the mount is full of broken Lines of Influence. This indicates disorders in the middle of the body, namely, the abdomen. The line running parallel to the Line of Saturn indicates a comfortable financial position.

Fig. 31D (Left)

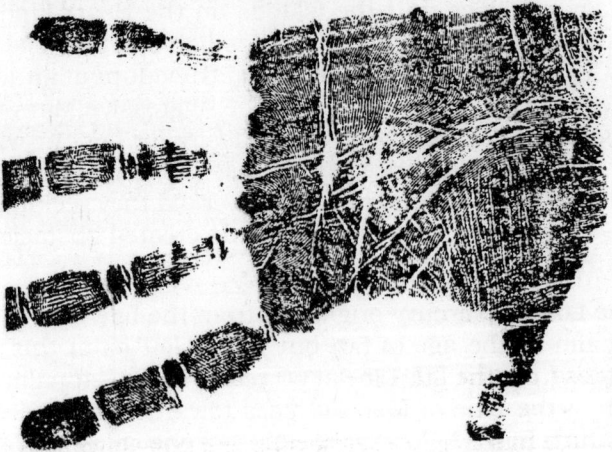

Fig. 31C (Right)

All the Secrets of Palmistry

The Line of Mercury in both the palms, the Mount of Jupiter and the defective Heart Line — all point to the fact that she is fond of eating but suppresses her desire because her stomach does not function as it should. Her unfulfilled desire for recognition tends to exacerbate her stomach disorders. Between the the age of 50-60 years her stomach trouble would get aggravated. The woman says that chronic dysentery is the root cause of all her problems. Remedies to correct the defects of the lines of the palm can help to improve her condition. Since the Life Line is without any breaks after the age of 60, her health problems would vanish after that. If the remedies suggested are followed, she can get some relief over a few months time.

The remedies suggested are — she should wear a copper ring in the ring finger to offset the effect of an underdeveloped Mount of Mars. Digital postures should be recommended for strengthening the heart and also to counter the evil effects of the Line of Mercury and the Line of Saturn. She should also look at her palms the moment she wakes up.

While taking leave, the client should be told that she would not face any health problems after the age of 60 and that she would remain mentally healthy till the end of her days. Though there would not be any new source of income during the period of her 60 to 80 years of age, she would not feel any financial crunch because of an adequate income from the old sources and her own habit of thrift. She would have a nice time insofar as health and recognition due to fame is concerned and that if remedial measures were taken, her future difficulties would be taken care off and positive results would follow.

Handprint in *Fig. 31-CD*

Handprints in the figure in the adjacent page belong to a 26-year old young man. Like most clients of his age, he had come with questions concerning material progress and marriage.

You can see from a cursory glance at the handprint that the palms do not have any criss-crossing of lines. There are a limited number of vertical lines, indicating a clear head and a balanced mind which is at peace with the world.

The mounts do not appear on a handprint and we had noted their peculiarities along with the other signs on the palms. Let us now find the effect of the other signs on the hand before we discuss to the lines.

The Aggressive Mars and the Mount of Moon are under-developed. The Mount of Jupiter and the Mount of Venus are well developed. The other mounts show a normal state of development. All the fingers are inclined towards the middle finger and both the phalanges of the thumb are of equal length. The skin of the palms is flexible and the setting of the fingers resembles an arch.

The flexible skin of the palms indicates an accommodative nature. The equal length of the two phalanges of the thumb is a sign of a balance between thought and action, which presages material progress. All the three fingers are inclined towards the middle finger which accentuates the quality of Saturn — sobriety and sagacity. The setting of the fingers, which resembles an arch, also speaks of a successful man with a balanced mind. The underdevelopment of the Aggressive Mars speaks of a peace-loving man. Normal development of the Defensive Mars indicates that this man would not lose heart in the worst circumstances. The underdevelopment of the Mount of Moon speaks of less imagination but more of pragmatism. The overdevelopment of the Mount of Venus is proof of a strong desire for marriage and heightened sexuality, but because there is no cross on the Mount of Jupiter near the Life Line, there can be no early marriage.

There are two Lines of Marriage or Sexuality — one appears at the age of 21 or 22 and the other at 28 years. The man must have rejected a marriage proposal which came to him at the age of 21 years because the standard of living of the family seeking an alliance with him was not up to his expectations.

But the position of the Line of Saturn arising from the Mount of Venus and going upward, indicates that his expectations would be fulfilled. Marriage at 28 years is indicated and the bride would be according to his requirements.

The other mounts are normally developed which is an indication of good fortune.

A positive feature of the palm is the Life Line which, branches out, with one going towards the Mount of Jupiter. The time at which this happens according to the Life Line is between the ages of 18 and 20 and which points towards his ambitions. That was the time when one or the other of his ambitions got fulfilled. There are Lines of Worry on the Aggressive Mars, but the line which intersects the Life Line appears at the age of 25. But it does not affect the Life Line in any considerable measure which means that any problem, if there was, has been removed. A well-defined and deep Life Line points towards good health.

The Life Line forks into two branches at the end — one of which goes towards the Mount of Moon. The fork which goes to this mount is longer than the main line, leading to the desire for foreign travel or migration to another country. The desire will get fulfilled.

A Travel Line originating from the percussion of the palm proceeds towards the middle of the palm telling that a long voyage is on the cards.

The Head Line originates away from the Life Line meaning that the person is used to getting his way, particularly because of his self-confidence. The Head Line is short in the right palm and long in the left, revealing that the man uses his brains excessively. The short Head Line in the right hand indicates that he should not overwork his brains but eat food which strengthens the brain and practice the digital posture that strengthens the Head Line.

The Heart Line is defective, but we would come to that later.

The Line of Mars is at a distance from the Life Line and is short. Being away from the Life Line predicts delay in marriage and that it would be shortlived because the man would have to make progress without support from any quarter.

There are two Lines of Saturn in the left palm — one

originating from the Mount of Moon and the other from the Mount of Venus. At first impression, the line coming from the Mount of Moon is a branch of the Head Line going towards the Mount of Moon. But a close look removes that impression. Beyond the Head Line, the Line of Saturn gets help from the Line of Sun which is indicative of success between the ages of 35 and 55.

The Line of Saturn stops after the Heart Line, but the double Line of Sun continues. We can interpret it to mean that after the age of 55 the man will not have any new source of income, but the old ones would continue and he would earn fame. But that time is far away at present and in the intervening years the length of the Line of Saturn could increase.

The Heart Line originates in the right palm from the Mount of Jupiter and in the left from a point between the Mounts of Jupiter and Saturn. It is the hallmark of a kind and sympathetic man.

The Heart Line is like a twisted rope and has islands over it, indicating emotional troubles for the man. He lavishes love on others but does not get any in return. That leads to mental anguish. It is because of such emotional shocks that the Heart Line has become defective. He should be advised to practice digital postures recommended in the previous chapter for correcting the faults of the Heart Line.

In the left hand there are two ordinary lines connected to a broken Girdle of Venus, while there is a small mark on the right palm. It is because of the pragmatic disposition of the man that the Girdle of Venus does not develop. From others signs on the palm one can conclude that this faint mark of the Girdle of Venus would vanish one day.

The sum total of all the signs on the palms of the person is that he is lucky. If digital postures recommended for correcting the faults of the Head Line and the Heart Line are practiced, the situation would improve because the faults would vanish over time.

XXXII

Important Note

The author has given broad outlines on the principles of palmistry and in Chapter XXXI he has explained how to practice it. As an aid to the practice of the craft, two handprints have been included in the that chapter. If you have diligently studied the earlier chapters and mulled over them, you are now qualified to read the palms.

A novice would have some difficulty in understanding the significance of the lines and other signs on the palm. If you find yourself in such a position, there is no reason to lose heart because your difficulties will disappear gradually and you would succeed in reading various palms and in understanding the significance of the lines.

Only one reading of a work on any science is generally not enough and you must, therefore, study this book again and again. You must also read other books, a list of which is given below:

1. *Palmistry, How to Master It*, by Dayanand

2. *A Hand Book of Scientific & Practical Palmistry* by Dayanand

3. *Fifty Handprints* by Dayanand & Nisha Ghai

4. *Palmistry Guide* by Nisha Ghai

While making your predictions to a client, always remember to give him hope and do not say anything which will dishearten him. If the signs of his palm are disappointing, you can tell him that just as there are medicines for all disorders of the body, there are remedies to improve your luck. Disappointment can turn into hope if the measures to remove the defects of the lines are vigorously pursued. The remedies for those defects have been given in Chapter XXX.

May God grant you success in all your endeavours.

Part-V

A New Concept
(A Clue to Physiologists to Study Human Nature through Palmistry)

XXXIII

Link Between Palmistry and Physiology

While moving around in society, I have observed that some people are fond of solitude while many others dread this seclusion and cannot exist without a large circle of acquaintances. There are some people who lead their lives according to the ethical principles of life while some others feel no qualms in violating these principles for personal gains.

Some persons are aggressive by nature, while contrary to them, some are docile and entrusting by nature. Some persons are devious and some innocent. A few are leaders by nature while most prefer to be followers.

With the help of psychology and study of physiology and anatomy, I have learnt that secretions from the endocrine glands play an active role in arousing feelings like sexual, anger, fear, etc. and that these glands are controlled by the central nervous system. The control centres for the sensory organs, like the eyes, ears, nose, taste, pain, etc., are already known to exist in the brain but I could not locate the control centres responsible for differences in human nature, either by reading books on physiology or anatomy.

Science has revealed that chromosomes and genes are responsible for differences in human nature but when I could not find any information on how and through which organs of the body the chromosomes and genes activate the basic nature of man, my curiosity led me towards the study of palmistry.

During the practice of palmistry (hand reading) I learnt that signs on the hands (chirognomy) convey about man's basic nature while lines on the palm (chiromancy) indicate the ups and downs a man will undergo in his life. Since I could find the control centres responsible for differences in human nature by studying the signs present on the palms, I am presenting herewith a description of this particular aspect of palmistry in this chapter. Subsequently, based on my study of anatomy, I'll present my hypotheses.

According to chirognomy, the palm is divided into nine parts. These parts have been called mounts. Details about these mounts are given in Chapters XII and XIII of this book. On discovering the link between palmistry and physiology I give here the brief descriptions of these mounts as ready reference. The fingers of the hand are responsible for enhancing or suppressing the powers of the mounts situated at their base. The importance of the thumb is distinctly separate from the mount located on its base.

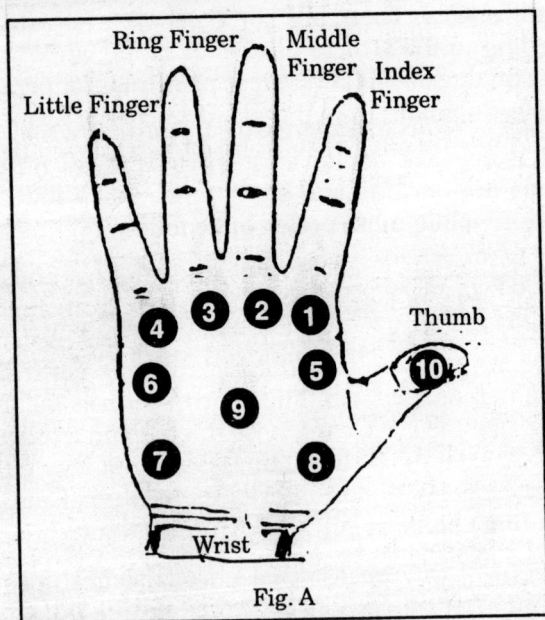
Fig. A

After studying the palms of thousands of persons, I have come to the conclusion that the mounts on the palms and the characteristics of the fingers present a true picture of a person's basic nature. According to my experience, this picture has proven correct for 90 per cent of the people. I explain through *Fig. A*, the point as to which mount and which finger on the palm presents which particular aspect of man's nature.

All the Secrets of Palmistry

In *Fig. A*, the position of Mount No. 1 (Mount of Jupiter) conveys the amount of ego present in a person. If this mount on the palm of a person is well developed, then it shows his desire to be a leader. If the finger emerging from this spot, and which is called the *index finger*, is longer than normal, then this characteristic of his nature gets enhanced. If the index finger is smaller than normal or if this mount is flat, then this characteristic declines. Such persons lack the desire for excellence and find it easier to be followers.

Mount No. 2 (Mount of Saturn) in *Fig. A* conveys a person's analytical powers. Normally this spot is depressed but the *middle finger* that emerges from this spot is longer than the other fingers. If the middle finger is equal in length to its adjacent fingers, then the person's analytical powers are less. Persons with the middle finger longer than normal are introspective by nature and fond of solitude.

Mount No. 3 (Mount of Sun) in *Fig. A* conveys the extrovert and ambitious nature of a person. If the mount is raised, this person has a powerful ambition. The finger emerging from this site, called the *ring finger*, enhances this aspect of his nature. If this spot is depressed and the ring finger is smaller than normal, then he lacks ambition.

Mount 4 (Mount of Mercury) in *Fig. A* depicts the practical nature of a person. If this mount is raised, the person gives importance to his own gains. The *little finger* emerging from this site is smaller than all the other fingers. If this finger is longer than normal or is crooked, then the person is smart and clever practically.

If Mount No. 5 (Mount of Aggressive Mars) in *Fig. A* is well developed, the person is arrogant by nature. If this mount is depressed, then the person's nature is to get subjugated rather than to subjugate. He quickly hands over whatever power he possesses.

If Mount No. 6 (Mount of Defensive Mars) in Fig. *A* is well developed, the person has immense patience. He does not get disturbed under difficult circumstances. But if the mount is depressed or is plain flat, then the person gets agitated and worried under adverse circumstances.

Mount No. 7 (Mount of Moon) in *Fig. A* conveys the

imaginative power of a person. Imperfect imaginative power makes the person into a daydreamer. Superior imaginative power is called the power of intuition. If this mount is highly developed, the person's intuitive power is high. If this area is depressed, this characteristic of intuition shows a marked decline.

Mount No. 8 (Mount of Venus) in *Fig. A* depicts the vitality and sexual power of a person. If this area is flat, these characteristics decline but if this mount is developed, there is an increase in these characteristics.

If Mount No. 9 (Mount of Mars) in *Fig. A* is well developed, the person is brave. He does not accept defeat in times of difficulties. If this mount is depressed, the person shows lack of fighting spirit in facing the difficult circumstances.

Mount No. 10 in *Fig. A* is called the *thumb*. If the thumb is longer than normal, the person is intelligent and desires to rule. When the thumb is smaller than normal, the power of a person's intelligence and the desire to lead decline.

I want to clarify here that I have talked about human nature and temperament as revealed by the level of development of each mount. Innumerable types of temperaments are revealed by a combination of mounts present at other spots on the palm.

An example is related to No. 10 on the thumb. A thumb longer than normal conveys sharp intelligence and desire to rule. To learn in which field — arts, politics, world of crime, etc. — a person with such a long thumb will use his intelligence, we need to study a combination of mounts at other places on the palm. A description of such a combination is available in this author's book entitled *A Hand Book of Scientific and Practical Palmistry*.

Information on the 10 mountsites is responsible for differences in human nature. A strange coincidence helped me to locate the behaviour control centres in the human body responsible for differences in temperaments. I was engaged in research in connection with a book I was writing on the psychology of sex. During this period I came across a book entitled *Human Physiology*.[1] I found some clues in the introduction given in the book regarding the central nervous

All the Secrets of Palmistry

system. On linking these clues with the signs on the palm (chirognomy), my curiosity was aroused. By consistently pondering over my findings, I came to the conclusion that there was a strong link between certain centres of the central nervous system and the signs on the palm. By identifying the missing links between these connections, answers to queries regarding the differences in human nature was found.

References to centres related to motor and sensory organs are provided through illustrations in the above-mentioned book and so is the relation between the control centres in the brain and the somato-sensory area. (Its illustration is given ahead). Since human nature is concerned more with the sensory than with motor organs, only the aspects related to the sensory organs are being highlighted through *Fig. B*.

Details of the Sensory Centres in Brain

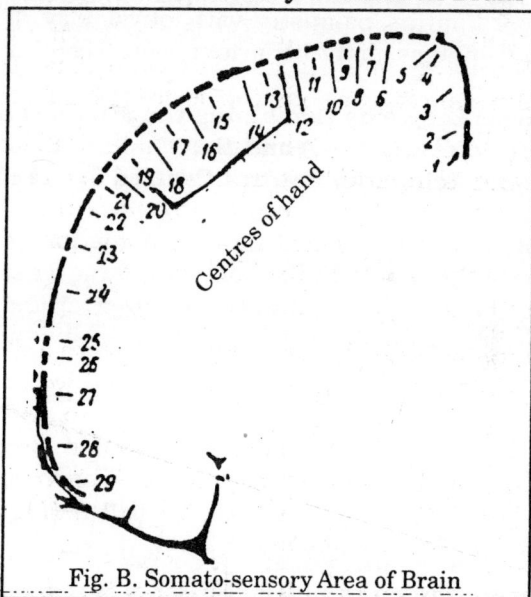

Fig. B. Somato-sensory Area of Brain

The numbers in Fig. B stand for the following:
1. reproductive organs, 2. toes, 3. feet, 4. legs, 5. hips, 6. trunk, 7. neck, 8. head, 9. shoulders, 10. upper parts of the arms, 11. elbows, 12. lower part of the arms, 13. wrist, 14. palm, 15. little finger, 16. ring finger, 17. middle finger, 18. index finger, 19. thumb, 20. eye, 21. nose, 22. face, 23. upper lip, 24. teeth, 25. lower lip, 26. gums and jaws, 27. tongue, 28. not known, 29. internal organs.

In this figure the centres between points No. 13 to No. 19 are related to the wrist, palm, thumb and fingers, while the other centres are related to other parts of the body.

The areas/mounts given in *Fig. A* of this Chapter are related to palmistry. In palmistry, the palm has been given importance while the fingers of the palm are treated as extensions of these mounts. However, the fingers have been given greater importance among the sensory centres of the brain as revealed by *Fig. B*.

The mounts marked on the palm in *Fig. A* reveal the different types of nature a person possesses. The centres of the brain in *Fig. B* were identified after a careful investigation of the brain and the objective of these studies is to identify and accordingly remove any disease that may be afflicting the body.

By coordinating palmistry with physiology, I wish to present my findings on the behaviour control centres in man.

Hypothesis Drawn by Combining the Findings of Figs. A and B
Probable Behaviour Control Centres in the Brain

Centre No. 13 in the brain is related to the wrist. Among the positions on the hand, the closest point to the wrist is No.7, (Mount of Moon) which conveys the power of imagination while position No. 8 (Mount of Venus) displays the vitality and sexual power in man (*see Fig. C*).

Hypothesis: On studying the Centre No. 13 in the brain in *Fig. C*, I found that one part conveys the imaginative power of the brain while the other part refers to the sexuality of a person.

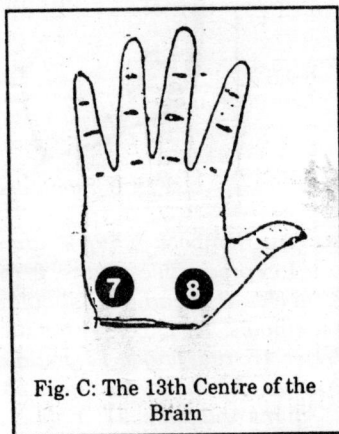

Fig. C: The 13th Centre of the Brain

All the Secrets of Palmistry

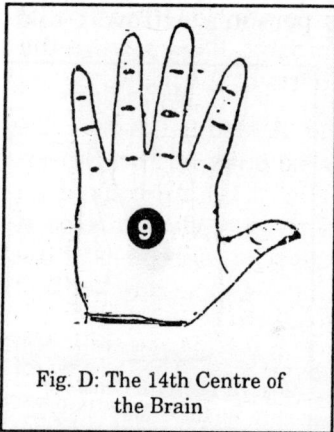

Fig. D: The 14th Centre of the Brain

In *Fig. B*, Centre No. 14 is concerned with the Plain of Mars. In *Fig. A*, the centre of the palm conveys the degree of courage present in a person (*see also Fig. D*).

Hypothesis: On studying the Centre No. 14 of the brain, the person's courage can be gauged.

Centre No. 15 of the brain is related to the little finger of the hand. The closest point to the little finger of the hand is Mount No. 4 (Mount of Mercury) which conveys the person's practical nature. The nearest point to No. 4 is No. 6 (Mount of Defensive Mars) which reveals the amount of patience present in a person (*see Fig. E*).

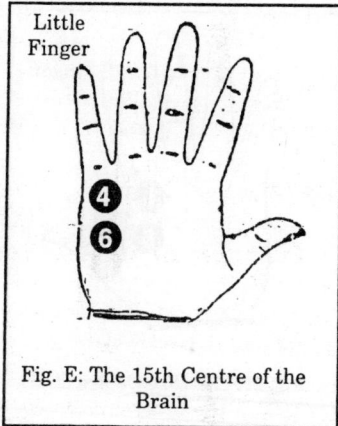

Fig. E: The 15th Centre of the Brain

Hypothesis: On investigating Centre No. 15 of the brain, one can learn about the practical nature of a person and the amount of patience present in him.

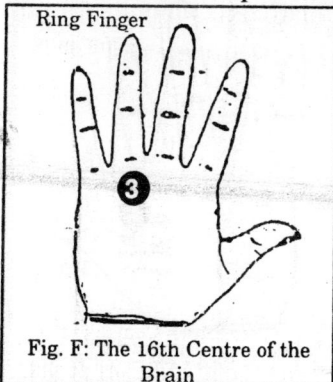

Fig. F: The 16th Centre of the Brain

Centre No. 16 of the brain is related to the ring finger. Centre No. 3 (Mount of Sun) is at the base of the ring finger and conveys the degree of ambition and extrovert nature present in a person (*see Fig. F*).

Hypothesis: On investigating Centre No. 16 of the

brain, one can learn about the person's extrovert and ambitious nature.

Centre No. 17 is related to the middle finger. The base of the middle finger (Mount of Saturn) conveys the introvert nature and analytical power of the person (see Fig. G).

Hypothesis: On studying Centre No. 17 of the brain, the analytical powers and the introvert nature of a person is revealed.

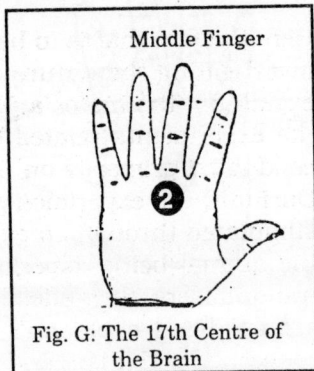

Fig. G: The 17th Centre of the Brain

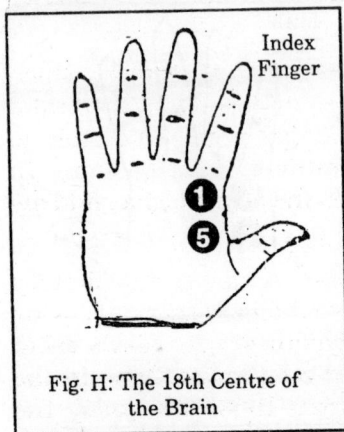

Fig. H: The 18th Centre of the Brain

Centre No. 18 of the brain is concerned with the index finger and Centre No. 1. The base of this finger (Mount of Jupiter) tells about a person's level of pride and desire for leadership, while Centre No. 5 (Mount of Aggressive Mars) below Mount of Jupiter conveys the person's arrogance (see Fig. H).

Hypothesis: On studying Centre No. 18, one can learn about a person's ego and his tendency to dominate.

Centre No. 19 of the brain is related to the thumb. The thumb conveys the degree of intelligence present in a person (see Fig. I).

Hypothesis: On investigating Centre No. 19 of the brain, a person's intelligence can be gauged.

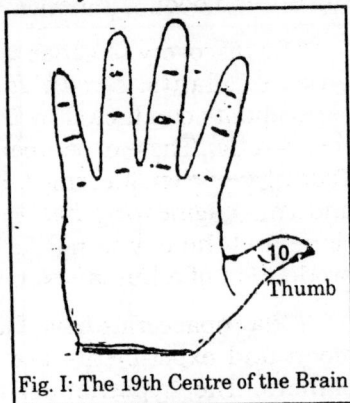

Fig. I: The 19th Centre of the Brain

All the Secrets of Palmistry

Some Observations on Analysing the Hypothesis

Here the fact that is to be accepted is that the procedure of investigating the nature of a person is more difficult than examining the motor and sensory organs. This is because the experiments related to the sensory organs have been conducted primarily on frogs, mice, rabbits and monkeys. During these experiments, the particular sensory organ is stimulated through an electrical current to see its effect on the animal being experimented upon. Moreover by using tranquillisers, their effects are observed. But in our case, we are studying a person's nature/temperament, which is concerned with man, and this could be his introvert nature, ego, intelligence, etc. Such experiments need to be carried out on human beings.

Nevertheless we find that the centres of memory which are concerned with man have been discovered in the brain. This raises hope that it may one day become possible to discover the centres responsible for differences in temperaments in persons provided the physiologists find my hypothesis logical enough.

It is quite probable that this dream may seem a fantasy but today's space rockets and invention of robots are living proofs of such a fantasy. The hypothesis of today's robot (mechanised man) was presented for the first time in the play *R.V.R.* by Karal Chapek (1890-1938) and today the science of mechanised robots in the form of humans has been developed. So far it has become possible to penetrate the human body and perform surgery on any diseased part.

The discovery of genes has led to the cultivation of new types of plants. Credit for this discovery goes to the experiments conducted by the Austrian priest, G.J. Mendel (1822-1884). These experiments were conducted on pea-pods. Today genetic engineering falls under the category of science and this engineering has led to the production of sheep's clone and the day is not far when it may even lead to the production of a human clone.

Today spacecraft have facilitated landing of man on the moon and experiments are underway to reach the other planets. The hypothetical theory of the spacecraft was presented in a fantasy entitled *From the Earth to Moon* by French writer, Jules Verne in 1873. Subsequently, novelist H.G. Wells (1866-1946) gave birth to a new category of science fiction in the world of novels. The well-known novels, *The War of the Worlds* (1898) and *War in the Air* (1908) by Wells were like prophecies of today's spacecraft. The theory behind launching a spacecraft with the help of a rocket before becoming free from gravitational pull of the earth was put forth in his novels by H.G. Wells.

The purpose of all this description is to say that by holding the thread of the signs present on the hand and as described in palmistry, those centres of the brain can be discovered which are responsible for the differences in human nature/temperament. If this hypothesis sounds logical to physiologists, then a new branch of physio-palmistry will take birth.

Finally, I conclude this chapter with the words that discovery of every new scientific invention begins with a hypothesis, even though it may take centuries to give shape of scientific reality to the hypothesis.

Bibliography

1. E.Babsky, B. Khodorov, G. Kositasky and A. Zubikov: *Human Physiology*, Vol. 2, pp 282, 285. Edited by E.B. Babsky, memberof the Ukrainian Academy of Science; translated by Yuri Shirokov T., edited by N.C. Creigliton and published by MIR Publishers, Moscow.

⬡ DIAMOND POCKET BOOKS PRESENTS

ASTROLOGY, VAASTU, PALMISTRY & RELIGION BOOKS

HEALTHS Books

David Servan Schreiber (Guerir)
❑ The Instinct to Heal
    (Curing stress, anxiety and depression
    without drugs and without talk therapy)
M. Subramaniam
❑ Unveiling the Secrets of Reiki
❑ Brilliant Light
    (Reiki Grand Master Manual)
❑ At the Feet of the Master (Manal Reiki)
Sukhdeepak Malvai
❑ Natural Healing with Reiki
Pt. Rajnikant Upadhayay
❑ Reiki (For Healthy, Happy & Comfortable Life)
❑ Mudra Vigyan (For Health & Happiness)
Sankalpo
❑ Neo Reiki
Dr. Shiv Kumar
❑ Aroma Therapy
❑ Causes, Cure & Prevention
    of Nervous Diseases
❑ Diseases of Digestive System
❑ Asthma-Allergies (Causes & Cure)
❑ Eye-Care (Including Better Eye
    Sight) Without Glasses
❑ Stress (How to Relieve from Stress
    A Psychlogical Study)
Dr. Satish Goel
❑ Causes & Cure of Blood Pressure
❑ Causes & Cure of Diabetes
❑ Causes & Cure of Heart Ailments
❑ Pregnancy & Child Care
❑ Ladie's Slimming Course
❑ Acupuncture Guide
❑ Acupressure Guide
❑ Acupuncture & Acupressure Guide
❑ Walking for Better Health
❑ Nature Cure for Health & Happiness
❑ A Beacon of Hope for
    the Childless Couples
❑ Sex for All
Dr. Kanta Gupta
❑ Be Your Own Doctor
    (a Book about Herbs & Their Use)
Dr. B.R. Kishore
❑ Vatsyana Kamasutra
❑ The Manual of Sex & Tantra
Dr. M.K. Gupta
❑ Causes, Cure & Prevention of
    High Blood Cholesterol
Acharya Bhagwan Dev
❑ Yoga for Better Health
❑ Pranayam, Kundalini
    aur Hathyoga
Dr. S.K. Sharma
❑ Add Inches
❑ Shed Weight Add Life
❑ Alternate Therapies
❑ Miracles of Urine Therapy
❑ Meditation & Dhyan Yoga
    (for Spiritual Discipline)   95.00

❑ A Complete Guide to
    Homeopathic Remedies
❑ A Complete Guide to
    Biochemic Remedies
❑ Common Diseases of Urinary System
❑ Allopathic Guide for
    Common Disorders   1
❑ E.N.T. & Dental Guide (in Press)
❑ Wonders of Magnetotherapy
❑ Family Homeopathic Guide
❑ **Health in Your Hands**
❑ Food for Good Health
❑ Juice Therapy
❑ Tips on Sex
Dr. Renu Gupta
❑ Hair Care (Prevention of Dandruff & Baldness)
❑ Skin Care
❑ Complete Beautician Course
    (Start a Beauty Parlour at Home)
❑ Common Diseases of Women
Dr. Rajiv Sharma
❑ First Aid (in Press)
❑ Causes, Cure and Prevention
    of Children's Diseases
Dr. R.N. Gupta
❑ Joys of Parenthood
M. Kumaria
❑ How to Keep Fit
Dr. Pushpa Khurana
❑ Be Young and Healthy for 100 Years
❑ The Awesome Challenge of AIDS
Acharya Satyanand
❑ Surya Chikitsa
Dr. Nishtha
❑ Diseases of Respiratory Tract
    (Nose, Throat, Chest & Lungs)
❑ Backache (Spondylitis, Cervical
    Arthritis, Rheumatism)
❑ Ladies Health Guide
    (With Make-up Guide)
L.R. Chowdhary
❑ Rajuvenate with Kundalini Mantra Yoga
Manoj Kumar
❑ Diamond Body Building Course
Koulacharya Jagdish Sharma
❑ Body Language
G.C. Goyal
❑ Vitamins for Natural Healing
Dr. Vishnu Jain
❑ Heart to Heart (with Heart Specialist)
Asha Pran
❑ Beauty Guide (With Make-up Guide)
Acharya Vipul Rao
❑ **Ayurvedic Treatment for**
    Common Diseases
❑ **Herbal Treatment for**
    Common Diseases
Dr. Sajiv Adtakha
❑ Stuttering & Your Child (Question-Answer)

Books can be requisitioned by V.P.P. Postage charges will be Rs. 20/- per book.
For orders of three books the postage will be free.

⊙ DIAMOND POCKET BOOKS

X-30, Okhla Industrial Area, Phase-II, New Delhi-110020, Phone : 011-51611861, Fax : 011-51611866
E-mail : sales@diamondpublication.com, Website : www.fusionbooks.com